Lost Restaurants of CENTRAL OHIO & COLUMBUS

Lost Restaurants of CENTRAL OHIO & COLUMBUS

CHRISTINE HAYES AND DOUG MOTZ

Foreword by Liz Lessner

AMERICAN PALATE

Published by American Palate
A Division of The History Press
Charleston, SC
www.historypress.net

First published 2017

Manufactured in the United States

ISBN 9781625859143

Library of Congress Control Number: 2017953981

For our mothers, Betty Hayes and Mary Motz.

CONTENTS

FOREWORD

It is my own memories of Columbus's lost restaurants that inspired me to become a restaurateur. Central Ohio's long winters push us indoors for inspiration, conversation and celebration over drinks and food (yes, in that order!).

It was in these lost restaurants that a diverse community of food service workers, barkeeps, neighbors, hungry people and foodies became family while breaking bread and toasting one another goodnight, sometimes every night. We patronized these spaces for lots of reasons beyond food; they provided us comfort, hospitality and respite from the rest of the world. It's why you never saw a television in Surly Girl Saloon; we wanted to be an escape.

As a Columbus lost restaurant alum, I am proud of my peers and grateful we got to grow up together. While the restaurant industry is competitive, the restaurant owners were often the best of friends, collaborating often to give charitably, throw parties and lift each other up. That story of our collective Central Ohio restaurant family supporting one another is realized best in the chapter celebrating Haiku and how so many of us came together to support Rachel Widomski, who was run over by a patron skipping out on a hundred-dollar tab.

I'm proud of my former business partners and their ongoing ventures: Tim Lessner at Tip Top, Carmen Owens at Grass Skirt and Marcy Mays at Ace of Cups. We all remember the lost restaurants that inspired us and are grateful that so many are being documented here.

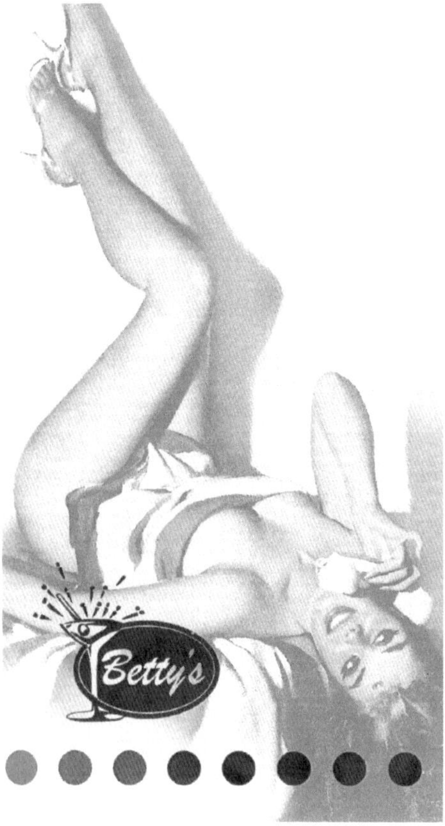

Betty's menu cover. *Courtesy Jim Ellison.*

The restaurant business is hard, and most people just don't get it. One person ripping you off can close a restaurant. The city can take away your parking lot, like it did at Tip Top for a month. You can have a bad, snowy winter, and it can lead to ruin. Trust me, I've made a lot of enemies, but I've always been forthright and honest about the situation at hand.

People have asked me if these books make me feel bittersweet. In fact, I look back on all lost restaurants with a sense of pride and awe. I'm lucky enough to say I was there. When Doug and Christine interviewed me about the closing of Betty's for *Lost Restaurants of Columbus*, I'll be honest that it was a cathartic experience to sift through all those memories again. But the "Lost Restaurants" books are the closest thing to being there, celebrating the endless nights and days of our lives. To so many of us, these restaurants hold our happiest memories and, for me, my youth and my most ridiculous dreams.

How many engagements were made at Rigsby's? How many prom nights and homecomings were celebrated in train cars at Victoria Station? How many anniversaries were celebrated at the Bexley's Monk? And how many family birthdays were spent at the venerable Clark's Dining Room?

We may never know the answer to any of those questions, as each lost restaurant holds so many of our own milestones. If you're at all like me, you wear your memories of lost restaurants like your favorite T-shirts from your favorite rock concerts. Old school takes on a new context here; you really had to have been there for the borscht at the Russian Tea Room or the time the lights went out at Ricky's Galaxy Café!

So it is my real hope that you'll read through these stories and that they may bring up treasured memories or even inspire you to have a new perspective the next time you go to your favorite neighborhood haunt for a bite. The men, women and in many cases families who ran these places did it out of love, and I invite you to sit back, get comfortable and enjoy a trip down memory lane.

—Liz Lessner
Lost Restaurateur of Columbus

ACKNOWLEDGEMENTS

Many thanks to the Acorn Bookshop Nuts, Maria Alexander, Ricky Barnes, Richard Baumann, Mark S. Brackney, Sonny Brockway, Chuck Capuano, Nora Chalfont, Doral Chenoweth, Thomas Clark, Augustine M. Cosentino, Gale Douglass, Jim Ellison, Bret Gandee, Becky George, Jerry Glick, Mark Gordon, Nick Gore, Bob Grove, Randy Headley, Charles Hedges, Donna Herb, David Hetzler, Arnett Howard, Bob Judson, Mary Beth Kanatas, Ted Kanatas, George and Joan Kasotis, Charles and Grace Langstaff, Karen Klingbeil LaValley, Pat Lewis, Walt Lindeboom, Jim Loeffler, Todd Long, Sandy Bean Lynch, Suzanne Kanatas Mardas, Dick and Harriet McClish, George and Diane McCoy, Sue Snouffer Kuhn Melvin, Sam Merkle, Martha Johnson Miller, Tim Miller, Elizabeth Moras, Michael Motz, Carmen Owens, Karen Kanatas Park, Jim Girves Paul, Felix and Sally Pedon, Kevin Pica, Todd Popp, Emily Prieto, Dana Navin Schultz, John Vollmer, Linda Vollmer, Matt Voltolini, Jeff Wasserstrom, David Webb, Bill Weidinger, David Wiggins, Ed Wolf and Helen Yee.

And to our invaluable, fabulous research specialists: Mary Ann Perine and Brenda Bellis of the Greater Buckeye Lake Historical Society, Aaron O'Donovan of the Columbus Metropolitan Library, Natalie Fritz and Kasey of the Clark County Historical Society, Mary Rodgers of the Clintonville Historical Society, Susan Logan of the Delaware County Historical Society, Jenn Lusetti of the Licking County Historical Society, John McPherson of the Logan County Historical Society, Phylis Miller of the Morrow County Historical Society, Darlene Weaver of the Pickaway County Historical Society, Beth Weinhardt of the Westerville Historical Society and *all* the reference librarians of the Old Worthington Library: gold stars!

Introduction

THE MEMORY OF A MEAL

Writing history is elusive; obtaining that one last fact or photograph is often as frustrating as finding that one book that's perfect for a person in the bookstore.

We have enjoyed giving talks on volume one of *Lost Restaurants of Columbus*. We've tried to include in this, the second volume, the restaurants most asked about when our talks conclude. The most-asked question: "Why do restaurants close?" with the corollary, "I wanted the ____ [Kahiki, Jai Lai, etc.] to last forever."

The answer is the firestorm of red tape surrounding a restaurant: lawyers and litigation, insurance, parking, partners, plumbers, permits and taxes. Flood, fire and fatigue figure in too. In the middle of all this is a chef who just wants to feed people and make them happy.

Trends of eating sometimes make the grand dames of restaurant fame seem old-fashioned, unless nostalgia is curated carefully. Neighborhoods deteriorate or get too popular; when it becomes dangerous to park or parking gets scarce and also expensive, the restaurant loses faithful customers.

Food supplies get more expensive; one restaurateur closed because he didn't want to raise his prices. He knew that would be the end of it—so he ended it himself. One can sense the lonely nights of decision weighing on a restaurant owner's mind. Owning a restaurant isn't a job; it is a lifework. And that goes for the most lavish restaurant down to the diner and drive-in. In a kinder, gentler world, everyone would listen to the same radio station and frequent the same local hot spots. Each scene would have its own following.

AIU Grill Liquors. *Courtesy Kanatas family*.

Explorer's Restaurant. *Courtesy Christine Hayes*.

Cork 'n Cleaver ad. *Courtesy Doug Motz.*

The cruising scene, around Jerry's and BBFs and Emil's and Don's and everywhere, was just that—a *scene*. This was not "vintage." This was not "oldies but goodies" on the radio. This was the *real thing*. Sons of World War II vets had their first cars, and they wanted to be *seen*. Just reading the blogs of today dedicated to old restaurants, it is obvious that for some people this was the highlight of their lives.

We remember the food and how good it tasted. Perhaps it was the ambience, the company and the newness of every food trend.

Restaurants are lost only when no one remembers them.

We have tried to include a spectrum of sentimental Central Ohio favorites and to go farther afield—to those places families and weary travelers stopped at and became delighted by and stopped at again and again.

So—enjoy, remember and try a recipe or two.

Chapter 1

DINERS

The Elmwood Restaurant

1965–1970

2177 West Dublin-Granville Road, Worthington

The Elmwood Restaurant was a little gem in Linworth started by Fred Snouffer and Maxine Snouffer. Elmwood was the former name of Linworth, now a part of Worthington. The name changed in 1910 due to the misrouting of mail intended for Elmwood Place in Hamilton County. The town of Elmwood, lying halfway between Worthington and Dublin, had its new name created from the last syllable of Dublin and the first syllable of Worthington.

Fred Snouffer was born in Linworth and lived there his entire life, along with a bevy of close Snouffer relatives.

The Elmwood featured daily specials of comfort food that cost exactly one dollar, including a beverage and three cents of tax. Because Linworth was experiencing a great deal of growth at the time (as it is again at the time of this writing), Maxine Snouffer wanted construction workers to be able to walk in with a dollar bill and enjoy a hearty, hot meal. Each special included an entrée and two side dishes. Meat loaf, Johnny Marzetti, fried chicken, pork chops and ham with cabbage were familiar menu items. Homemade chili and vegetable soup were standard fare, along with scrumptious made-from-scratch desserts. Fred's mother, Frankie Snouffer, and teenage daughter,

Sue, baked the pies using their crust recipe made with lard. Wedges of fruit pie were a quarter, and cream pies (homemade butterscotch, lemon meringue and coconut cream) were thirty-five cents. Another Worthington High School class of 1965 graduate, Esther Brooks Hunter, was a cook. (Sue Snouffer Kuhn Melvin, Esther Brooks Hunter and Christine Hayes are all part of this illustrious class and meet monthly with others of this distinction at various Worthington restaurants for fine meals and conversation.) Sue, like her father, has lived most of her life in and around Linworth.

The daily Elmwood Restaurant menus were created on a portable typewriter, and neighborhood kids washed the dishes and bussed the tables.

The site of the hometown Elmwood is now Dublin Cleaners. The restaurant had one more owner before it closed (perhaps because the construction workers had finished their jobs). It is to be noted that two doors to the west of the former site of the Elmwood is Cameron's, noted Columbus restaurateur Cameron Mitchell's first restaurant. Mitchell has gone on to a huge restaurant empire since founding Cameron's, but fortunately for Linworth diners, he likes to keep his first small hometown place as it was.

Harold's Third & Town

1939–1980
88 East Town Street, Columbus

Third & Town at (Mound and High)

1980–1992
346 South High Street, Columbus

In the 1920s, Harold Wasserstrom's father ran and owned a malt store at 74 East Town Street that was frequented by home-brewers during Prohibition. When Prohibition ended, he opened up Joe's Place in the same location until moving to the corner of Third and Town in 1939, when he bought the building and opened up the Intersectional namesake grill with his son Harold as a partner.

Harold's son Jeff shared these memories of the place:

> *Dad's cabbage rolls were not only the best but probably the biggest. Customers would ask how many cabbage rolls they should order and be told one would be enough. Once they received their hearty-sized cabbage roll, their eyes would light up and* [they would] *say something like, "I see what you mean!" Dad served daily specials, of which cabbage rolls were just one of these. Think they were Friday's special, along with one of my favorites: macaroni and cheese.*

The location at Third & Town had been a bar since 1902. At that time, it was called the Turf. During the 1920s, when women were discouraged from drinking in public, they would be served in a private upstairs "wine room." Additionally, since the location was so close to the bus stop that served commuters going from downtown to Beulah Park, horse players would place their bets at the restaurant.

Harold Wasserstrom at Third & Town. *Courtesy Jeffrey Wasserstrom.*

That crowd of horsey folks would continue to call Third and Town a home away from the track until 1980, when the Capitol South Community Urban Redevelopment Corporation announced it would raze the building. Harold Wasserstrom was paid $119,000 for the building and about $25,000 in moving expenses but relayed to *Dispatch* reporter at the time that "the move alone would cost him $75,000."

Harold couldn't find another building to purchase, so he rented a floor at 346 South High and moved the Town & Third to Mound and High, where its sign likely confused many passersby until it closed for good in 1992.

Chapter 2

NEIGHBORHOOD HAUNTS

FAR EAST

1930-1942
ADDRESS UNKNOWN EAST MAIN STREET, COLUMBUS

1941-PRESENT (RENAMED WING'S)
2801 EAST MAIN STREET, COLUMBUS

YEE'S

1967-1983
2525 EAST MAIN STREET AND 2974 EAST BROAD STREET, COLUMBUS

In the late 1920s, George L.W. Yee came to Columbus and, to the best of our knowledge, opened the first Chinese restaurant here. Prior to starting Far East, he had worked as a waiter, for he was personable and spoke excellent English.

George was born in Ton Shan, Guangdong Province, China, on November 5, 1900. His grandfather Jin Jang Yee immigrated to San Francisco in 1885. Jin Jang Yee worked in railroad detail, mining and farming until he was delivering produce in San Francisco and was killed in a horse cart accident.

Far East Restaurant. *Courtesy CML.*

Because the deceased must be returned to the homeland according to Chinese custom, George's father went to San Francisco to carry out this task. Later, he, too, immigrated to Phoenix, Arizona, in 1895.

George's mother raised four children by herself in China, which was common practice in those days. George attended elementary school and high school and learned English proficiently enough to teach others. George married and had two sons; he supported the family by teaching. In 1921, his first attempt at immigrating did not take; he was jailed and sent back to China because he replied wrongly to a question. In 1922, he succeeded and joined his father in Phoenix. Instead of helping his father in his grocery store, George performed farm work, which he did not like. At that time, George turned to restaurant work. He most likely came to Columbus through another family connection.

It was not long before he and partner Walter Ming opened Far East. George was the front-of-the house manager and bartender, and his partner was the chef. They imported weekly grocery shipments from San Francisco such as snow peas, fresh mushrooms, wonton wraps and spring roll wraps. They grew their own bean sprouts in the kitchen. They hired fine cooks from Chicago and New York. Soon they expanded and moved to a new, larger space. They could not obtain a liquor license in Bexley, so they moved to 2801 East Main Street in 1941 and built a twelve-thousand-square-foot restaurant that today is known as Wings.

George was able to send money back to his family in China. He went home to China in 1927 and not again until 1937. Two more children were born. The Japanese invaded Nanking at this time; George returned to Columbus and could not return to China for twenty years due to immigration laws and war. He continued to send money home for the children's educations and to

Far East/Max's ad. *Courtesy Doug Motz.*

buy houses and land. George sent money to the Chinese government to help the war efforts against Japan. Because of the war, the family and George had no communication between 1940 and 1945.

After the war, George sponsored the immigration of his nephew Wing Yee from China in 1946, and Wing worked at Far East. Finally, in 1962, George's son Peter (Sum Yin) Yee, his wife and four children, including

George's granddaughter Helen Yee, arrived in Columbus from Hong Kong. George and his partner parted after forty-five years in the restaurant business together.

George opened Yee's; he brought many of his cooks with him, and they featured both Chinese and western-style dishes. George's nephew Wing eventually leased the Far East restaurant from the owner and changed the name to Wing's, as it is today, noted for its fine cuisine and expansive collection of connoisseur single malt scotch, courtesy of Kenny Yee.

In 1974, George's son Peter took over the operation of Yee's. George and his wife moved temporarily to Vancouver to be with his daughter Sum Fong. But they missed their many friends in Columbus and moved back. Peter died of a heart attack in 1982, and his wife took over the restaurant for a year or so. The business was sold in 1983; at this writing, it is Billy Lee's Restaurant. George died in 1983 and is buried next to his wife in his beloved Columbus. Many of the Chinese restaurants in Columbus can trace their roots and employees back to George Yee's influence.

The Arlington Monk

1983–1987
1677 West Lane Avenue, Upper Arlington

The Blind Monk/Bexley's Monk

1984–2010
2232 East Main Street, Bexley

It was always the dream of George and Diane McCloy's friend John Larger to open a restaurant, and so the group borrowed some money and initially opened up the Arlington Monk as a fun piano bar and steak house. The idea was good, but the restaurant didn't last very long in Upper Arlington and by July 1987 had been replaced by a China Dynasty restaurant.

Fortunately, the group also had a place in Bexley that was initially called the Blind Monk. Diane explained that it was derived "from Dom Pierre Pérignon, the famed Benedictine monk and cellar master of the Abbey of

Bexley's Monk ad. *Courtesy Doug Motz.*

Hautvillers in Champagne, France. To ensure the highest-quality grapes were selected for his wines, Dom would taste and select grapes without knowing the source vineyard. This crucial first step of what became known as the *Méthode Champenoise* led to a revolution in the production and quality of sparkling wine. Over time, references to these 'blind tastings' led to the misconception that Dom Pérignon was blind."

It was a terrific restaurant with an unfortunate name, and in late 1987, the name was changed from the Blind Monk to Bexley's Monk after being picketed by the blind and their advocates for what many felt was a slight on their lack of sight.

It quickly gained a terrific reputation as a wonderful steak and seafood restaurant and a place to see and be seen in Bexley. Regulars had their names inscribed at the bar with brass nameplates. Even Bexley's longtime mayor, David Madison, got top billing in the private Madison dining room. There was entertainment every night, most notably the piano stylings of Sonia Modes, who as of this writing is still a fixture at Bexley's venerable rat pack–era haunt, the Top.

George said that he and Bexley's Monk business partners Frank and Don Casto spent "too much money" making the place feel elegant and homey, but the gorgeous wooden interior matched the tasty offerings of Chef David Wolf, and the Monk was regularly listed as one of the top ten restaurants in Central Ohio.

After George and Diane McCloy took a trip with Betty Rosbottom to Napa Valley in California in 1991 (Betty was the originator and director of the beloved Columbus Cooking School La Belle Pomme from 1981 to 1995), the Monk was able to bring in Franklin County's first wood-fired pizza oven. Many patrons flocked to the restaurant to try the tasty delicacies. That venture to wine country also inspired the Monk to add a raw seafood bar.

They also regularly began hosting get-togethers for the YPO (Young President's Organization). "They were a ball!" stated Diane.

In 2009, the business changed hands from George McCloy, but that ownership was short-lived, as the new owners, General Manager Remo

Stripe and Chef Ben Geltzer, closed the Monk for good in 2010. Barrel 44 came in for a very short while but also closed quickly in 2013 to make room for a new Giant Eagle that would open on the site of the Bexley City Hall.

As of this writing, Bexley City Hall is located at the site of the Monk.

Emil's Steer Inn

1959–1977
4484 East Main Street, Columbus

Emil Windmiller was born on a farm on South High Street in Columbus and, before opening Emil's, lived on a farm on what was once the Ohio State University's farm on Lane Avenue.

Emil's was a nationally known drive-in and popular hangout for teens as well as families in Eastmoor and Whitehall. Kids who really loved the place affectionately called it the unfortunately nicknamed "Slime" (Emil's spelled backward).

Emil's served typical diner fare, such as hamburgers and milk shakes, but was known for the pickle platters that would arrive at the table before the main dishes arrived. Emil actually made all the pickles himself. In addition to the pickles, the baked goods were wildly popular, and many believe that the Russian rum cream pie was only served at this restaurant.

Emil's postcard. *Courtesy Christine Hayes.*

Emil's interior postcard. *Courtesy Christine Hayes.*

In 1977, Emil sold the restaurant to Chuck Capuano, and it became Capuano's for the next eleven years. The Capuano team smartly kept on the famous pie bakers, Eunice and Bea.

In later years, Emil Windmiller returned to his farming roots and became known for keeping his then country place of 150 acres in Pickerington along Route 256 as a wild goose sanctuary. As of this writing, that sanctuary is now home to a Kroger.

The Fontanelle Restaurant

1963-2003

166 Graceland Boulevard, Columbus

The Fontanelle, with its fresh yellow-and-blue exterior, was a beckoning sight in the Graceland Shopping Center for decades. It was the creation of

Left: Fontanelle ad. *Courtesy Christine Hayes.*

Right: Fontanelle matchbook. *Courtesy Christine Hayes.*

Robert Susi, who set high standards for cleanliness. On Saturday nights, his crew cleaned every aspect of the kitchen—floor to ceiling. The Columbus Health Department loved him!

The menu was Italian but also had steaks, seafood and frog legs sautéed in garlic butter. Susi wanted to create a "dining experience," with atmosphere and polite service, before that became a hallmark in many places. He had a prime rib special on weekends, when the place was really busy. He wooed the businessmen of the area with terrific lunches and drew in families and couples at night with subdued lighting in his lush dining room and cozy booths.

Susi sold his restaurant after thirty-four years in April 1997. As of this writing, the north side of the Graceland Shopping Center has been totally rebuilt; the Fontanelle would have been where the row of small stores sits just west of Michael's craft store.

Merkle's

1896–1930

400 North High Street in Union Station, Columbus

Ben Hayes wrote, "Merkle's generation of Columbusites would say it was the best restaurant Columbus has ever had." Peter Merkle opened the lavish dining room at the train station in 1896. The walls were marble, the waiters wore tuxedos and the meals were served on bone china. Trains brought in fresh seafood and meat daily. Merkle's was known for steaks, lamb chops, roast beef, whitefish and fresh oysters from Chesapeake Bay. Henry Feuillerat, the Merkle's chef originally from Toulouse, France, would say, "There are no fiddle strings in Merkle's steaks."

The restaurant had two sides, one less formal; there, tall silver coffee urns stood inside a U-shaped counter. During the most bustling train traffic years, Peter Merkle never closed. Two of his sons, Edward and Bill, helped maintain a twenty-four-hour schedule. A midnight custom for Columbusites was "to be seen at Merkle's." Well-dressed customers would jostle through the coffee shop after downtown theaters closed.

Merkle's was famous for its custom-blended coffee (sold in stores under the Merkle's and CiBon brands). This coffee created night owls wandering around Columbus—the Dawn Patrol! Customers would then head back out to clubs and casinos, including Pat Murnan's.

Big Ten football meant fans on excursions in parlor cars and Pullmans, all of whom needed to spend some money at Merkle's en route. They wanted lunch at the front tables.

Peter Merkle & Sons duplicated the success of the Columbus restaurant in rail stations throughout the Midwest. Peter went on to be one of Columbus's most prominent businessmen, focusing not only on restaurants but banking and real estate as well. Merkle's closed in 1930, due to the Depression. Peter Merkle's descendants continued in the food business with Merk's at the corner of East Main and Kenwick, as well as a diner in what is now the Arena District. The coffee company also continued under Edward's guidance.

The site of Merkle's is now the Columbus Convention Center.

Peasant on the Lane

1981–1994
Lane Avenue Shopping Center, Upper Arlington

After working at Federated Department Stores as a vice president of operations in the restaurant division, Walt Lindeboom and his co-worker Don Walsh decided they wanted to do something on their own. Dan Reinike, who ran the restaurant Peasant Stock in Dayton, was going to go in with them but decided to drop out before the venture began.

Walt shared, "We received excellent training from Mr. Charles [Lazarus] in merchandising and in customer service. He would stress to us that the 'impossible just takes a little bit longer,' and that was the philosophy we started when we opened up the restaurant."

When asked about the name, he said that they wanted to "try to tell people where it's at," and since Dan already had Peasant Stock in Dayton, they thought, *why not Peasant on the Lane?*

The Grumpy Gourmet wrote of the décor, "Peasant on the Lane is a most pleasant establishment, sectioned off into levels with lots of dividers and wide aisles. The decor is a blend of Spanish stucco and California freshness with much polished wood and shiny brass. There are enough florals, ferns and plantings to make you think you're in Franklin Park Conservatory."

Walt let us know that they "had excellent suppliers and our fish had to be fresh," and it was that freshness for their seafood that garnered Peasant many accolades. Frozen fish was never served on the menu. In fact, one of the hallmarks of the restaurant was that the menu did change daily, usually due to what seafood they were able to procure that day.

Walt developed a relationship with the M.F. Foley Company out of Boston while a student at the Culinary Institute of America in 1958 and maintained that trust throughout the time Peasant on the Lane was open. Fish would arrive in wooden boxes packed in ice fresh from the Atlantic, and diners always knew that the offerings would be as fresh as possible. One of the most popular dishes was a Cajun-style tuna steak that, according to Doral Chenoweth, would be coated in "an overdose of cayenne, a blasting of granulated garlic, white and black pepper, thyme, basil, salt."

Walt shared that people also came in for the extensive wine list. The restaurateur worked closely with Roger Gentile Wine Cellars, and Peasant was also one of the first places to offer wine by the glass.

Left: Peasant on the Lane ad. *Courtesy Doug Motz.*

Right: Peasant on the Lane matchbook. *Courtesy Doug Motz.*

Desserts were from the ovens of fellow Federated colleague and baker Teres Whitfield, who came to Columbus from Switzerland and as of this writing still owns the Swiss Pastry Shop, which continues to supply many desserts for local establishments. Among the favorites she created were Irish whiskey cake, triple-layer cheesecake and, as a nod to Lazarus's Chintz Room, a special pecan ball coated in her special Swiss chocolate sauce.

Lindeboom had time for fun, and as an avid Michigan State University alumnus working in the decidedly Buckeye country of Upper Arlington, he would always entertain the MSU cheerleaders and alumni when they were in town to play against the OSU Buckeyes. He also had a lot of fun on Bastille Day and would work up special French menus for Peasant.

Server Trish Nagy was a crowd favorite; diner Joan Frazier shared back in 1993 that Trish was always "well-groomed; friendly without being too personal; knows each day's menu and can describe dishes; brings coffee refills before you ask; constant attention to basket of rolls and butter; well-versed in wine presentation and service; can handle large, noisy, rough parties with aplomb; can cheerfully handle 'ladies who lunch' as they figure out combined checks to determine who owes what."

Walt's children also worked at Peasant on the Lane, including sons John, Rob, Rick, Stephen and Jamie, as well as daughters Heidi and Anne, who worked the coat room on weekends. The restaurant business must have really stuck with several of them, as John is executive chef at Willowbrook Retirement Center and Rick is executive chef at Rusty Bucket as of this writing.

Business was going very well for the restaurant, which consistently was considered one of the top places to dine by critics, but nature intervened to hasten the closing of this beloved place. On January 29, 1994, the roof of the Lane Avenue Shopping Center "cracked" due to severe weather. This roofing problem caused the temporary closing of thirty-eight businesses in the Lane Avenue Mall, including Peasant. Lindeboom tried to keep Peasant on the Lane open, and for a while there were even several umbrellas holding back rainwater from the leaky roof over the bar.

In March 1994, Peasant on the Lane announced it would not reopen and would work with other establishments to honor outstanding gift cards.

The Peasant space was taken over in October 1994 by the Bexley's Monk owners, Jack Cory, Steve Gifford and Ed Miller, and renamed Bistro Roti.

Walt went on for a short while to be a culinary consultant for Restaurant Consultants but ended up spending the better part of his career post-Peasant working with Glory Foods in marketing and product development. (Glory Foods president Bill Williams had worked for Lindeboom back in his Federated days.)

DRAGONFLY NEO V/TILL DYNAMIC FARE/ IZZY & MO'S DELI

2000–2016
245-47 KING AVENUE, COLUMBUS

In June 2000, a restaurant opened that fairly glowed from its sense of well-being. Dragonfly Neo V, the creation of dedicated couple Magdiale Wolmark and Cristin Austin, had minimalist elegance and sensuousness of good taste. They called their cuisine and hand-crafted beverages "Neo V," as in futuristic vegan. They prepared dishes with the freshest and healthiest of organic ingredients. They and their staff were always patient in explaining the nuances of the cuisine.

The large dragonfly sculpture lighting fixture was reflected by the long inlaid-tile iridescent bar and long, indented group table. In a *Short North Gazette* column, Christine wrote in August 2000: "My companion and I had

Magdiale Wolmark starting a kitchen garden at Dragonfly. *Courtesy Christine Hayes.*

nori spring rolls, risotto with citrus rind, papadou, hijiki seaweed, banana lime salsa; polenta with ginger figs, onions, olives, eggplant, tahini, grilled tofu, celery, and zucchini. And for dessert: hot strawberry and pineapple cobbler with lavender gelato."

The spirits were as exotic and organic as the food. Already a popular center for the neighborhood, the building had housed the bead and incredible import store Byzantium and the vegetarian King Avenue Coffee House. Dragonfly featured cutting-edge art on the walls and eye-catching advertisements, often with the couple's children depicted. At Comfest, the Dragonfly booth was housed at first in a silver spaceship-like entity, and then for many years they had a more normal booth along the eastern strip.

Cristin and Magdiale hosted Earth Day festivities, art cars, bands, children's activities, art shows in their side gallery, book signings, wine and spirits tastings and private parties. Soon they air-hammered the oil-stained pavement behind the restaurant and made an idyllic little organic kitchen garden. Some of their ingredients became even fresher.

Raen of Dragonfly Neo V. *Courtesy Christine Hayes.*

In 2011, they reinvented themselves as Till Dynamic Fare, still an organic restaurant but now featuring meat and fish of the highest organic order, as in grass-fed cows and wild-caught salmon. Hayes has a note from another column about enjoying pawpaw cocktails and wild-foraged black walnut caramel turtle tarts. Life was never dull at this King Avenue oasis!

In 2015, Till's little side-building, which had been a sandwich and "faster-food" bakery for a time before, with delicious Magdiale creations of sesame wraps and many other fanciful delights, was converted into a full-fledged, but still organic, Jewish delicatessen called Izzy & Mo's Deli. The deli was named for Magdiale's parents, who always came to Columbus for the annual Seder. Magdiale's father is a rabbi. The "third-wave deli" featured organic takes on blintzes, smoked fish, chopped liver, cured brisket and bagels, among other creative deli fare.

In 2016, the entire family moved to Ann Arbor and sold the building. At this writing, the site hosts the Angry Baker restaurant and the Bitter Barista coffee bar.

The Florentine Restaurant

1945–2016

907 West Broad Street, Columbus

This wonderful Franklinton restaurant held forth for seventy-one years, hosting family gatherings and wedding receptions and just plain good eating for generations of diners. The menu did not change much from the hearty Italian fare of its origins in 1945 under owner Tony Penzone; lobster ravioli with house-made vodka pasta sauce and eggplant Veronese were always favorites.

The slight changes were from booths to tables in the 1980s, and the two large wine barrels—one holding rosé and one holding red—were removed in the 1990s. When the third generation of family restaurateurs, Nick and Peter Penzone, announced they were closing just before Christmas 2016, there was a sad note to that holiday season.

During one memorable visit by Doug and his husband Todd Popp on a Thursday night in 1999 (Thursday night featured an all-you-can eat spaghetti and meatball special which Doug loved!), Doug ordered a house salad pictured on the menu with banana peppers. When his server brought the salad, it had the requisite lettuce, dressing, and tomatoes but no banana

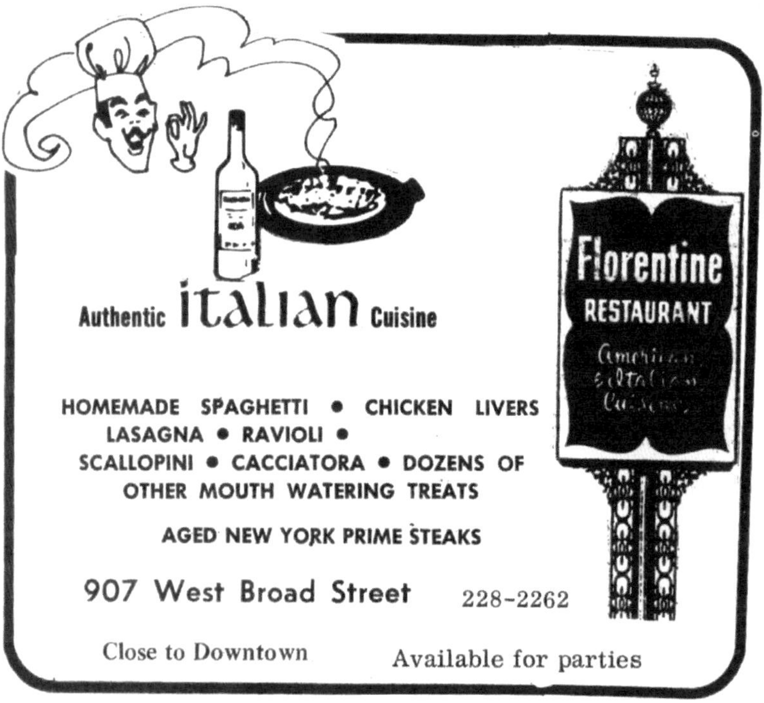

Florentine ads. *Courtesy Doug Motz.*

peppers, so Doug asked if those could be added, to which his server replied, "I'll gladly 'upgrade' you to banana peppers!" which has become a private joke with them ever since.

At this writing, the Robert Weiler Company has purchased the Florentine, with its 6,560 square feet of interior, and parking lot. They purchased it intact, with the dishes and furniture. The company is waiting to see if any restaurateur wants it, but it could be demolished if there are no takers. The Robert Weiler Company, in partnership with the Casto Company, is building 230 apartments on the nearby Scioto Peninsula. The Franklinton area is going through major changes.

Willard Restaurant

1925–1988
2282, 2270 and 2143 East Main Street, Bexley

Touchstone Café

1990–1996
2143 East Main Street, Bexley

The Willard Restaurant opened its door to the village of Bexley in 1925. At this time, it shared occupancy with Wentz Pharmacy across from Capital University at 2282 East Main Street. As of this writing, that space is home to a Graeter's Ice Cream franchise.

The restaurant was founded by Willard Wendt, who wanted the community to have a place where neighbors could sit down and enjoy a good home-style meal at an affordable price. He moved the restaurant twice early on, once to the northwest corner of Drexel and Main at 2270 East Main and then, according to Columbus Metropolitan Library records, to 2143 East Main in 1943.

The place gained a national reputation and following when Duncan Hines, then a restaurant reviewer, praised the food.

Becky George studied teaching at Capital University, and during that time, she was a server at Willard's from 1967 until 1971. She recalls that she was paid seventy-eight cents an hour plus tips and that there was an enormous handbook that all of the servers had to memorize:

> *It was mostly things like, serve from the right and pick up from the left. But I remember that we had to have perfect nail polish with no chips whatsoever or wear none at all. Additionally, we all had to wear the same type of pastel apron....*
>
> *Mr. Wendt and his wife, Billie, were very hands-on and would sit at a family table inside the restaurant. Their son Billy worked as a busboy when I was there. The manager was Mae Forrest, and she was a German immigrant who was a stickler for perfection. She would bring in lovely hand-carved wooden as well as hand-blown ornaments into the counter display during the holiday season and place them for sale.*
>
> *The signature dishes at the restaurant were broasted chicken and roasted turkey. There was a man named Gene who worked there whose job it was to roast the turkeys every day, and he would usually arrive around 4:00 a.m. to get them started. They also had a salad girl who prepared only salads and a baker who made all the pies, cakes and corn bread sticks and biscuits that we would bring out to the table when our diners were seated.*
>
> *We were allowed to have a free meal, provided it wasn't more than two dollars and twenty five cents, so I usually ordered the perch dinner or ground chuck. The side dishes all had interesting names on the menu, such as Blue Lake Green Beans or Our Delicious Cole Slaw.*
>
> *Besides the delicious food served in the restaurant, they also made all of their own ice cream, and folks could walk up to a separate carry-out area to pick up pints for sale. My favorite was always the mint chocolate chip because they used Maramor chocolates in it!*
>
> *During the holidays, we were very busy, and I remember having to work Thanksgiving as well as Christmas for a solid eight-hour shift with no breaks. The Wendts were always very generous, though, and inspired a great deal of loyalty not only from the college kids like me but from the career waitresses. As a bonus, besides a generous envelope of cash, the family would take all of us somewhere special. I remember going to Holiday on Ice at the Fairgrounds Coliseum with everyone!*

Wendt ended up selling the business in 1980 to Gary and Caroline Anderson. They ran it for eight more years, abruptly closing it in 1988. However, the restaurant wasn't shuttered for long, as the Touchstone Café opened up its doors at 2143 East Main Street in the fall of 1990.

Willard's. *Courtesy CML.*

The concept of Touchstone was unique. Servers in the place were differently abled individuals, and the not-for-profit would provide them with free training to learn a trade in the restaurant industry. Initially, the not-for-profit café had several high-profile partners. Wendy's donated all the kitchen equipment and furniture, White Castle donated $50,000 toward renovation costs and the Fifty-Five restaurant group's chef, Cameron Mitchell, created all the lunches and dinners. The Ohio Department of Development also contributed a $500,000-plus grant to cover salaries.

Executive Director Susan Berg stated, "We're providing people with the development skills that can change the quality of their life." The servers were chosen by referrals and stayed until they mastered their skills.

The restaurant attracted a great deal of attention, and seemingly some folks who stopped by were more interested in observing the trainees than eating the food. Former first lady of Ohio Janet Voinovich even stopped by in 1991 to serve up potato soup from a recipe handed down to her by her Grandma Zisha.

But like many new ventures, the Touchstone had money troubles. It failed to meet the original training goals set down by the state, and a succession of three managers in less than two years put increased pressure on the unique eatery.

Joseph Drury, Touchstone's vice president and a division vice president for Wendy's restaurant chain, shared another difficulty: friction among the leadership team. Board members are not shy "about saying their piece," Drury said. "Everybody is very outspoken."

Apparently, the friction didn't get much better, and Touchstone officially closed in July 1996. For a short while, it was owned by the Steak Escape chain and then changed hands again and became one of the last iterations of Fisherman's Wharf (see chapter 5).

The building was demolished in 2005, and as of this writing, the land is a parking lot across from Jeni's Ice Cream in Bexley.

Haiku

1999–2016
800 North High Street, Columbus

Su Lan

2000–2004
2894 East Main Street, Bexley

Bento GO GO

2003–2012
1728 North High Street, Columbus

Paul Liu already had a successful Chinese restaurant at Stone Ridge Plaza in Gahanna (China Gourmet) when he started his search across the country to find top chefs for his new restaurant, Haiku. He specifically searched in big cities with large Asian communities and was rewarded with a chef from Japan and one from Korea.

Haiku filled the spot of the short-lived restaurants Sweet Pea and Viva in the Short North as a sushi and Asian noodle restaurant exclusively. Liu was definitely surprised when, without any marketing or promotion, he had packed houses during his opening weeks in 1999.

In writing about Columbus's growing discriminatory tastes, Doral Chenoweth, aka the Grumpy Gourmet, wrote:

> *The number of Asian eateries here has grown to the point that we can become discriminating. Give credit to early entries such as Sapporo Wind and Restaurant Japan. Our appetite and acceptance of sushi has been refined to the point that our city now has a sufficient number of customers who seek out little places such as Haiku. Other Japanese restaurants may offer larger bills of fare, but none attempt such a bullseye focus on just two facets of Japanese cuisine: sushi and noodles. Haiku carries 14 variations of the latter.*

> *In the Haiku presentations, the more adventurous will note other Asian influences—pad Thai, for example. China comes into play with Singapore noodles, rice noodles with chicken in a light curry sauce. It appears this Japanese restaurant is fusion Asian. Japanese purists may differ with me, but I think Haiku's widely diverse noodles list will be the lasting attraction.*

At 1,800 square feet, Haiku was seemingly always bustling. In October of that first year, next-door neighbor Rupert's closed and allowed Haiku to expand to 5,000 square feet. Rupert's was a destination for take-away prepared gourmet foods.

One of the unique aspects of Haiku was that there was pencil and paper at every table for patrons to compose haikus while dining. Or they could read and admire the three-line, seventeen-syllable poetry of fellow diners that was displayed along the restaurant's walls.

Sushi soon came to dominate the menu, and lovers of the dish could dine on such fare as futomaki rolls, veggie rolls filled with oshinko, gobo root and kanpyo, kani rolls of crab leg and saba.

With Haiku doing well, Liu ventured out to Bexley in 2000 to open Su Lan in the former Cameron's Bexley location and Café Martinique prior to that at 2894 East Main Street. Su Lan opened as a French Vietnamese fusion restaurant and garnered a good following but closed in 2004 to be replaced by a place named "Singles."

A few years later, he also opened Bento GO GO on the OSU Campus at 1728 North High Street. Named for the Japanese boxed lunches, two-story Bento GO GO was a lively, vibrant café filled with techno beats, and it

Haiku. *Courtesy CML.*

had an upstairs sake bar, complete with instructions on sake etiquette. The popular eatery suffered a flood along High Street in 2004 but was able to do very well until closing in 2012.

Then on May 15, 2008, everything changed at Haiku. Michael Rose was dining at Haiku and left the restaurant drunk and high on cocaine without paying for his meal. Co-owner Julie Liu and bartender Rachel Widomski took off after him to get the $101 restaurant bill. Rose ran over them, causing Liu to have head injuries, a broken wrist, broken ribs and a broken collarbone and Widomski to have spinal cord injuries and paralysis from the waist down.

The entire Central Ohio restaurant community came together in support with fundraisers for the victims. Tommy Gallo of Gallo's Tap Room put together a twenty-two-bar tour named Bethel Backs Rachel to raise money for Widomski's many medical bills. Servers at Haiku and many other area dining rooms donated their nightly tips to her fund as well.

Michael Rose was charged with a five-count indictment on charges of aggravated robbery and felonious assault and was further indicted in August 2008 on charges of aggravated vehicular assault and two counts of failure to stop after an accident. In February 2009, Rose pleaded guilty to the many charges against him and cut a plea deal to half the time he would have spent in prison. He did receive a sentence of fifteen years.

In a statement to *The Other Paper* in September 2009, Rachel Widomski wrote the following:

> Amor fati.
>
> *I live to see the beauty in every occurrence. I do not believe in fate as absolute; contrarily it is our response to destiny that shapes our existence.*
>
> *I remember the day that they told me that I would not be able to walk again. I tried to cry, but couldn't. I already knew. I remembered the moment that it happened. I had already accepted it.*
>
> *My response was, "what's next?"*
>
> *I have faced much adversity in my short life of 29 years. Sometimes I feel as if I've lived the life of someone three times my age. It was these life vicissitudes that gave me the strength needed to overcome this incident.*
>
> *It has been 16 months of learning how to live again. I have had to relearn everything, even how to merely sit. The body will heal with time, but the mind must be strong to drive it.*
>
> *My December birthday brought about living without medical assistance. The New Year started my independent study at home. March brought about*

> *learning how to drive. In the spring, true to its nature, everything came full circle as I returned to OSU.*
>
> *There are many times when my body cannot keep up with my determination. I welcome and embrace those days, same as the accomplished ones. I greet each day with an open accepting soul, even the unpalatable ones.*
>
> *Not one day begins without overwhelming gratitude for every person who has touched my life in the passing months. I wish there was a word to describe my appreciation for this amazing community, which supported me, and my family, in such a dark hour. The largest honor I can give is to tell you all that you are now my family, and your compassion will never be forgotten.*
>
> *My legacy is not tragedy, but something more that has yet to be discovered.*
> *Truth and compassion,*
> *Rachel Widomski*

Further development in the Short North brought an end to the popular Haiku. Crawford Hoying bought the parcel in July 2016 and, as of this writing, has plans to build an 111-room hotel on the property. Haiku closed on December 10, 2016.

SURLY GIRL SALOON

2005–2015
1126 NORTH HIGH STREET, COLUMBUS

Surly Girl Saloon (SGS) at 1126 North High was opened in 2005 in the space previously occupied by the Downtown Connection, a predominantly LGBT sports bar. Opened as part of the Betty's family of restaurants, Carmen Owens was the true force behind the place. She recalls:

> *Among the three of us* [Elizabeth Lessner, Marcy Mays and Carmen], *we really wanted a place that was clearly female-owned, and we wanted the vibe to be comfy, cozy but also wanted people to know their place—it was very much a vibe of "this is our juke joint and our rules, deal with it or get out." And for the most part, I think people appreciated that.*

She went on to say:

> *One thing that most people don't know is that I have known the Lessner family since about '92. Tim and I dated for years in high school and after, and when we broke up, I basically told him that I was still keeping his parents and his sister, because they were like another family to me. We had all "grown up" together and had all worked in restaurants, both separately and with each other, for years. So, basically it was a bunch of bratty longtime restaurant peeps who just decided—let's open a bar together. And if we're gonna open a bar together, how do we make it awesome for other people like us?*

The location was chosen on the fringes of the Short North's northern end. Carmen explained that with SGS, Little Brothers and Skully's all clustered together, it created a weird rock-and-roll sweet spot around Fourth and High.

The concept for SGS came together at O'Reilly's over many plates of nachos and "pink drinks." The conversation went something like this: "Let's do an Old West vibe but with skulls! Like cowgirls in a brothel on a pirate ship?! Awesome!"

Carmen said the signature dishes came together because she liked salads that were more junk food than salads—really just piles of fried things and good cheese with lots of veggies.

> *I was tired of going to Barley's Smokehouse to get their salad (with dried cherries and walnuts and blue cheese—which I would put onion strings on, yum!), so I asked Liz to put something similar on the Betty's menu since I worked and ate there most nights, and that's how the Surly Girl Salad was born. Liz named it and just said, "No one knows it yet, but eventually it'll be promo for the new joint." And then one of the cooks made it into a wrap with turkey, and voila! The Surly Girl Turkey Wrap. So…when we finally worked on the real menu at Surly, I just said, well, Betty's can't have more Surly Girl menu items than we do; what if we put all that stuff on a pizza? Thus, the Surly Girl Pizza was invented.*
>
> *Initially, we had a tiny little all-electric kitchen with one and then two pizza ovens and some steam tables. So we only had a few options—we could make pizzas, warm up already prepped things like meatloaf or toast sandwiches. We figured we had to have a grilled cheese. And if we were going to have grilled cheese, we had to have tomato soup. So I recommended my favorite recipe from childhood: Campbell's Tomato*

> *Soup and milk, but less milk than it says to use. We upgraded it to half and half and added a little sriracha, but that's all our famous tomato soup was: Campbell's Tomato Soup from a can. And people loved it! I think because it tasted so familiar to everyone but they couldn't figure out why!*

The Super Supper trays were born out of Carmen seeing them in a place in Chicago that did TV dinners before SGS opened. She said it took her three years to find the trays but that they were really fun and she loved them.

She said her crowd was also a crossroads of people who weren't really OSU campus but weren't "fancy" Short North either. She explained that they were "people going to shows—everyone including Abercrombie, Wexner center staff [and a] place to take out-of-town guests for a sort of quirky, edgy, wacky experience."

When we asked her about what made Surly Girl Saloon so special, the memories came tumbling out like water trapped behind a dam for far too long:

> *The atmosphere was so dark and cozy but rowdy and fun. No TV, no clocks and all those chandeliers made it feel timeless in there. The decor was so over the top and had a weird goth-but-feminine feel to it. Pirates, skulls, lace, mirrors, a giant chandelier—there was something to discover every time you came in.*
>
> *Music was controlled by Marcy on jukebox (voted best jukebox even after we didn't have a jukebox). We had a "we reserve the right to cancel any song you play so don't play shitty music" sign from Marcy on juke—and she would do it if she didn't like what you were playing.*
>
> *Punk Rock Aerobics on Tuesdays for five years in a row…Marcy and Jen Burton taught the class every week.*
>
> *Open Mic Comedy on Wednesdays for eight years with Sean Somerville.*
>
> *We had Peeptinis on Easter. We were open on holidays like Christmas and Thanksgiving, so people would come spend their holidays with us every year. One year for High Ball, we dressed up as Pee Wee's Playhouse.*
>
> *Marcy's parents made the tables. Liz's mom and I spray painted all the scorpions on the "wallpaper." Liz's mom helped us design the main chandelier out of eight thrifted chandeliers, but as the electrician was wiring it, she asked if we could please afford to buy her two more chandeliers at Lowes please. We gave the folks at Byzantium a gift card and some cash to help us decorate it with all the beads.*

> *People always thought we were a gay bar. Something about the words "surly" and "girl" together, I think. I don't know. But we always said that anybody that wouldn't come 'cause they thought it was a gay bar wasn't welcome anyway. One of our original bartenders, "Bubbles," christened SGS a Pansexual Rock N' Roll Palace—and I always thought that was the best bar genre ever invented.*

When we asked about special recipes at SGS, Carmen reminded us that she had already shared the tomato soup one but insisted we write about cupcakes.

> *You have to talk about our cupcakes! Started as just chocolate-cayenne, but we had sooooo much fun making up cupcakes! Red velvet at the end were most popular, but we did a cupcake du jour: zombie cupcakes, beer cupcakes, booze cupcakes, bacon cupcakes, local lemon and lavender cupcakes for Michelle Obama when she was FLOTUS, mini cupcakes, and Cupcake Camp. Gah! I was obsessed with cupcakes because they're so cute. And you can get really weird with them. But I can't bake; Emily Clemons was our cupcake girl, along with Lara Ranallo, our last kitchen manager.*

She said that the closing of Surly Girl was hard but that when it closed in 2015, it really wasn't on the fringes any longer, and that was where she and Marcy and Liz operated best. Carmen shared:

> *I'm really happy about the life cycle of that bar. Though I know a lot of folks were sad to see it go, it was important to me to go out on a high note, and I hope people feel like it did.*
>
> *When we went in, twenty-four taps was almost unheard of, but by 2015, twenty-four taps was passé; like everyone had seventy-five drafts at that point. Our cocktail menu had long been based on a method of two to three ingredients and a funny name, and people wanted fancy cocktail bars. I refused to buy Surly Girl a muddler for like the first two years, and that still makes me laugh to think about. We put in—and paid off—a new kitchen, had stopped doing events long ago to focus on food and booze; redid the back room; we had attempted to break the world record for longest hula hoop upstairs; I had rented that space to a children's theater and then the SNBA and then CFL; I learned how to put on events from Cupcake Camp, to Parking Lot Blowout, to Halloween High Ball, how to open an art gallery (Gallery Upstairs with Jen Burton). I*

felt like I had tackled all the challenges that place had to throw at me, I was ready to focus on the new tiki bar that needed my attention. And the neighborhood was changing, maturing too. So it felt like a good time to say goodbye.

Anyway, the point is this whole thing is like a family. I'm sure you've heard that before about the restaurant business. But it really, truly is. From beginning to end, I'm proudest of the fact that we created a Surly Girl family and that those connections still exist even if the place isn't physically there.

I still tell my parents they should consider it their first grandchild. And then I say, "But isn't it great that I didn't have real babies because you can't legally just sell them off to the highest bidder when they're annoying ten-year-olds?" And we all laugh, but everyone knows I kind of mean it. About why I don't have babies.

And about what happened to Surly Girl Saloon.

In closing, she said she really wanted Surly Girl Saloon to be remembered "as a safe haven for a bunch of weirdos. And as a creative, empowering, rowdy, welcoming place."

As of this writing, the space is occupied by the Short North Parlor Room.

D'Ascanio's Distinctive Foods

1950–1980
3569 Cleveland Avenue, Columbus

One of Columbus's favorite neighborhood Italian restaurants, D'Ascanio's came straight from the Presutti family, as Eda D'Ascanio was a Presutti daughter. The former house sat in what is now a jumble of stores, apartments and auto repair shops but at the time was an undeveloped region. In the foreword of Mrs. D'Ascanio's cookbook (1952), Ben Hayes wrote, "In a large gracious mansion, centered in its own park, outside Columbus…a retreat as agreeable as Chianti."

This was not any old cookbook; it was called *Famous Recipes* and ran to 226 pages. In addition to the recipes, it included wine information, the history of Italian cooking, holiday tips and a children's corner. The cookbook was reprinted four times, through 1979.

Eda D'Ascanio went on to found the Palette Café at the Columbus Museum of Art, with the assistance of the Women's Board of Volunteers there. D'Ascanio's also had the Golden Putter at 1600 Northwest Boulevard, which is as of this writing a Donato's pizza shop.

The D'Ascanio's original site is, at this writing, Lee's Auto Repair, just north of Northern Lights Shopping Center.

Whole World Bakery

1978–2017

3269 North High Street, Columbus

Opened in the former Clintonville Bakery, Dan and Kim Otanicar started Whole World in 1978, essentially as a pizzeria, offering customized pizzas representing the flavors of many different nations of the world—thus the name Whole World—and a full bounty of vegetable toppings. The twenty-two-seat restaurant also served up a multitude of breads, bakery items and soups, including patron favorites five-grain loaf, butter bread, Hungarian mushroom soup, date bear paws (Kim's take on mincemeat) and oatmeal cookies.

Whole World was one of the first places in Columbus to offer up exotic pizza toppings such as pineapple, Oregon apples, sunflower seeds, fresh bananas, avocados and even coconut. It became known early on as a vegetarian place but actually did offer up such hearty fare as pepperoni pizzas and submarine sandwiches loaded with meat. It would likely come as a surprise to most casual diners to learn that at home, Dan and Kim regularly cook up meals such as boneless pork shoulder roast with ricotta cheese and chicken and noodle soup, "just like Mom made," said Kim. In 1992, the couple made the decision to have the menu go completely vegetarian, making it one of the first all-vegetarian restaurants in Central Ohio.

About eight years into the business, the couple toyed with the idea of selling the place but eventually decided to stick it out for the duration.

Whole World was also very popular on the festival circuit and was one of the first restaurants to regularly take the show on the road with booths and catering at local festivals like the Columbus Arts Festival, garnering many accolades as a crowd favorite.

On October 28, 2009, a kitchen fire closed the restaurant for several months. Here are the details from a July 6, 2010 *Columbus Dispatch* article:

> *On Oct. 28, a fire near one of the coolers destroyed the restaurant's heating, cooling and electrical systems and caused significant smoke damage in the rest of the interior.*
>
> *It could have been worse. Baker Maryellen Curran reported the fire before the blaze spread, and residents of the apartments above the restaurant were evacuated without injury.*
>
> *Otanicar thought he'd be open again by Christmas, but the repairs never seemed to end.*
>
> *"At first it didn't seem bad, but because of the location of the fire, it required a lot of repairs," he said. "It was a long eight months."*
>
> *About $50,000 later, the updated Whole World made its debut last week with a fresh coat of paint and new flooring, furniture, kitchen equipment and range hood.*

Fortunately, the signature Woodland mural of the Four Seasons above the bakery case was spared, and patrons were once again enjoying some of the finest vegan and vegetarian cuisine Clintonville had to offer.

However, seven years later in April 2017, the couple decided to close the landmark. "I absolutely adore the customers," said Dan. "It's just time."

As of this writing, the space is still unoccupied, awaiting its own next chapter.

RICKY'S GALAXY CAFÉ

33 BEECH RIDGE DRIVE, POWELL

GALAXY GRANDVIEW

1099 WEST FIRST AVENUE, GRANDVIEW HEIGHTS

LOST PLANET PIZZA & PASTA

680 NORTH HIGH STREET, COLUMBUS

EXPLORER'S CLUB

1586 SOUTH HIGH STREET, COLUMBUS

Ricky Barnes had been a celebrated sous chef at Lindey's and Rigsby's, getting noticed in particular in 1992 by Doral Chenoweth for his roasted potato soup with pancetta and rosemary while at Lindey's.

With his friend and fellow chef Jerry Burgos, he opened up Ricky's Galaxy Café in Powell. They named the restaurant for one of Jerry's favorite automobiles, the Ford Galaxy. Many called the place pan-ethnic because of the variety of influences on the food at Galaxy that included Creole, Brazilian, Mexican and lots of Cuban. When we chatted with Ricky about Galaxy, he was particularly proud that they "did vegetables and breakfast really well. We were the first to do black bean hummus, and nobody in town was really doing anything like that at that point in time. We really did the kind of food we liked to eat."

When the place first opened in May 1993, the pair each took home only fifty dollars a week in salary. "Our wives both had good jobs, and we had a landlord who was amazing to us, so we really kind of 'gave it away,' hoping that in doing so, folks would come back for more, and they did!"

Barnes went on to tell us:

> *We did lots of Cuban food, but we had no money and couldn't afford a deep fryer, so we had a double-sized crockpot and a Dutch oven. We used the crockpot as our "fryer" and then the Dutch oven as our warmer. When we finally started getting somewhere, we bought a walk-in refrigerator, but it was so small that the folks working with us called it the "peek-in."*
>
> *We called in lots of favors to open the place, and my neighbor Leonard Whitsetin did all the carpentry for us for free. But man, he was so great, he and his family always ate here for free. He then turned us on to an out-of-this-world plumber who did thousands and thousands of dollars' worth of plumbing for us for a song, and we did the same for him. He and his family always ate for free.*

> *We had the best staff in town. You know, it was the 1990s, and we had all of these hippie chicks who were so sweet and so fun to work with. I mean, people wanted to work for us, which was great because we were turning the dining room over four and five times a night.*

Galaxy became known for its fried plantains, vegetarian black beans and rice and serving breakfast all day on weekends.

During a power outage in 1995, the crew borrowed candles from the Powder Room shooting range next door and lit the place by candlelight. That was the start of a weekly tradition of dining by candlelight that proved very popular.

The Grandview restaurant came about because Mark and Tom Waggenbrenner were frequent diners and asked if Barnes would look at a property with them in Grandview; it became the Galaxy Grandview. Barnes recalled:

> *After we had been open a while in Grandview, when folks would camp out and not leave the place, I had a CD of Japanese disco music called* Shang Shang Typhoon. *All I had to do was put that on and gradually increase the volume, and that would finally drive out the diners who had stayed past our closing or their welcome.*
>
> *Sandy and Mark Woods were also good customers and asked what we wanted to do next. In 1996, I went to Chicago and had pizza at a place where they were serving it on cracker-thin crust, like a real Venetian pizza, and I told Sandy and Mark that that was what I wanted to do next. We went down and looked at the space, and that's how Lost Planet came into being.*

Lost Planet was known for its cracker-thin crust pizza and funky décor befitting the Short North in its infancy. Barnes really liked carnival sideshow artwork, thrift store finds and bright sunburst-style works.

Ricky shared, "It was more important to me to prove that I could do it. It was really more fun opening new places than running them."

Ricky got tired of the long drive to Powell and sold Ricky's Galaxy in 1997 to a group calling themselves the 33 Beechridge Drive Inc., made up of Martin Yetzer, Mark Gutantag and Trent Iguchi. By 1998, Ricky had sold all of his interest in the businesses and moved to Taos, New Mexico. The Grandview place was sold to Mike Purdum, who had plans to initially open something similar to his Old Bag of Nails pub in

LOST PLANET
PIZZA & PASTA

680 North High Street
Phone 614-228-6191

APPETIZERS

☺	**Roast Vegetable Yogurt and Black Bean Hummus** with Pizza Croutons	4.00
	Lost Planet Caesar Roast Garlic Dressing Tossed with Romaine Lettuce	3.75
☺	**Mixed Lettuces** with Red Wine Vinaigrette	3.75
	Artichoke Dip Basil, 3 Cheese Gratin with Pizza Croutons	4.75
	Crabcakes with Jalapeno Mayonnaise	4.25
	Roasted Garlic Potato Pancake topped with Gorgonzola and served on a Chianti Wine Tomato Glaze	3.75
	Roman Bread This bread is brushed lightly with Olive Oil and is covered with Garlic Herbs, Red Onions, Calamata Olives and Melted Gorgonzola Cheese	5.25

PIZZAS

	Our Pizzas Come Large and Extra Large	LG-14"	XLG-14"X22"
	Pepperoni & Cheese	8.50	11.00
	White Pizza Roast Chicken, Caramelized Onions and Fontinella Cheese	8.50	11.00
	Roast Vegetable with cheese	8.00	10.50
☺	without cheese	7.50	10.00
	Mushroom with Three Cheeses	8.00	10.50
	Mozzarella & Fontinella (no red sauce)	7.50	10.00
	Blackened Chicken Caesar Pizza Blackened Chicken and Crisp Romaine with Caesar Dressing and Parmesan Cheese	8.50	11.00
☺	**Roast Sweet Corn** with Roma Tomatoes, Caramelized Onions, & Low Fat Mozzarella	7.50	10.00
☺	**Spinach** with Caramelized Onions, Roasted Garlic, Feta Cheese, Red Wine Vinaigrette	8.00	10.50
	Spinach with Red Sauce, Fontinella Cheese, Feta Cheese, Roma Tomatoes Red Onions and Roast Corn	8.50	11.00
	Taco Pizza Cheddar Cheese, Assorted Peppers including Jalapenos, Red and Green Peppers, Ground Beef, Red Onions and Chipolte Salsa.	8.50	11.00
	Roast Chicken on a Tomato Basil Chutney with Cumin Mozzarella and Roast Corn	8.50	11.00

PASTAS

		HALF	FULL
☺	**Linguini** tossed with Shrimp, Bay Scallops, Feta Cheese and Roma Tomatoes in a Cured Lemon Basil Vinaigrette	6.50	10.50
☺	**Penne** with Pan Roast Vegetables, Lemon, Garlic, and White Wine	6.00	9.75
	Rotini with Seared Pork Tenderloin Pork tenderloin with rotini and mushrooms, corn, tomato, black olives in a savory chipotle cheddar cream sauce	6.50	10.50
	Rigatoni with Roma Tomatoes, Roast Garlic and Spinach in a Gorgonzola Tomato Cream Sauce	6.00	9.75
	Smokey Chicken Penne with Jalapeno, Chicken, Caramelized Onions, and Mozzarella & Parmesan Cheeses in a Special Smokey Cream Sauce	6.25	10.00
☺	**Rigatoni** with Chicken, Roasted Vegetables, and Special Soy Broth	6.25	10.00
	Ravioli Stuffed with Smoked Chicken, Asiago, and Green Onions with Roast Corn, Chipotle Sauce, and a Jalapeno Pineapple Salsa	6.25	10.25
	Ravioli Stuffed with Six Cheeses in an Oven-dried Tomato, Artichoke Heart Relish	6.25	10.25
	Not Lasagna Pasta Penne, Pepperoni, Tomatoes, Jalapeno with a Marinara Cheese Mix	6.25	10.25

NEW EMPLOYEE MENU

Brought to you by the ingenious members of The Lost Planet family

(For a limited time - Subject to change)

APPETIZERS

Employee's Favorite # 1 - Ricky's Cheesy Garlic Lover's Bread
Start off your meal with our delectable Italian Bread. This bread is has been delicately prepared with a special Dipping sauce and a tasty 3 cheese garlic mixture that will please your palette!
Enjoy! $4.25

PIZZAS

Our Pizzas Come Large and Extra Large	LG-14"	XLG-14x22"
Employee's Favorite # 2 - Tangy Tonya's BBQ Pizza Wow, A true Lost Planet special – A special pizza with a special mango BBQ blend with Mozzarella Pineapples, Jalapenos, Peppers and Red Onions	8.25	10.50
Employee's Favorite # 3 - Southwestern Pizza Geraldo Style The southwest hits the Planet. A mixture of Oil, Mozzarella, Cheddar and Fontinella cheeses with Black Beans, Tomato, Red Onions and a touch of cumin	8.25	10.50

PASTAS

	HALF	FULL
Employee's Favorite # 4 - Big Al's Super Summer Slam Special A pasta for the people! A penne pasta that includes Jalapenos and Italian Sausage, Marinara, Green Peppers and Caramelized Onions	6.50	10.50
Employee's Favorite # 5 – Kathy's Boathouse Special A unique seafood blend that includes Rotini, Shrimp, Scallops, Tomato, Spinach, 3 cheeses, Mushroom in a Creamy Alfredo Sauce. A must have for all seafood lovers!	6.50	10.50

DINNERS

	Nonni's Roast Chicken with Rosemary, Soy, Mushrooms, Sherry and Linguini	8.00
☺	**Grilled Fish** with Linguini, Seared Vegetables, and Lemon Basil Drizzle	9.00
☺	**Sicilian Pizza Dinner** Enjoy Sicilian Pizza Lost Planet Style, includes Pepperoni, Red Sauce, Caramelized Onions, Jalapenos, Mozzarella and a side of Red Wine Salad	6.95

DRINKS

Sodas	1.25	Coffee	.95
Hot Tea, Iced Tea	.95	Milk	.95
Juice	1.25	Lemonade	1.25

☺ - low fat or no fat

Top: Lost Planet menu. *Courtesy Jim Ellison.*

Bottom: Lost Planet employee menu. *Courtesy Jim Ellison.*

Worthington. The guys to whom Ricky sold the Powell business lured him back to assist with it. They changed the name to Ricky's, but he left after six months and took a job at OSU as a chef with a buddy he worked with in the 1980s. "I was their trouble-shooting guy," he told us.

That lasted for a while until Barnes became interested in senior living operations and became a consultant to lots of those facilities. He said, "There's a real move to home cooking there, and I love teaching folks how to do that."

However, Traci Studer called him back to check out a place in Merion Village that eventually became the Explorer's Club. They co-owned it together 50/50. Explorer's Club also became well known for Latin, Cuban and breakfast foods, with the Cuban French toast being a solid performer. Barnes said, "Traci sold me on it as a way to use up stale bread, and it really is so easy to make and delicious!"

But again, that didn't last long, as Ricky explained to us that he "can't really work with anybody and it worked out great for all of us."

As of this writing, Ricky commutes weekly back and forth to West Virginia, where he consults with a senior living facility. When we asked what he would say about the restaurant, he said just go and buy great stuff from Traci at the truck that, as of this writing, he operates at Zauber Brewery in Grandview.

Chapter 3
DOWNTOWN FAVORITES

Top of the Center

1971–1977

100 East Broad Street, twenty-fourth floor, Columbus

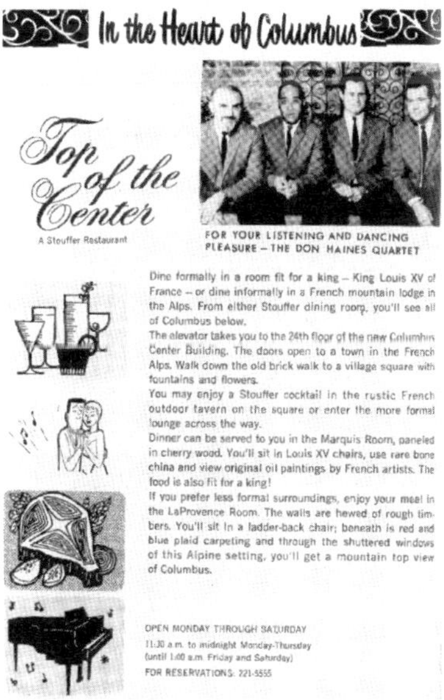

Top of the Center ad. *Courtesy Doug Motz.*

Stouffer's opened Top of the Center in 1971 on the top floor of the City National Building, later the BancOne Building and then Chase Bank. This was the second-tallest building in Columbus at the time.

The restaurant billed itself as "The High Spot in Columbus" with a balloon-with-baskct logo. It advertised dancing on Friday and Saturday evenings, with private dining facilities available. The classy British motif and the cherries flambé prepared at your table could not save it, however. Soon thereafter, the chain opened the Stouffer's at the University Inn, with its connecting pool covered with an inflatable dome for winter swimming.

Top of the Center ad. *Courtesy Doug Motz.*

At this writing, the University Inn area has become the Olentangy Shoppes strip mall, anchored by a Denny's. Stouffer's opened One Nation in 1977 in the thirty-eighth floor of the One Nationwide Building and closed the Top of the Center. At this writing, the top floor of the Chase Bank Building is empty.

The Fire Mark

1973–1990

471 East Broad Street (460 Oak Street), Columbus

In a Ben Hayes column in the *Columbus Citizen-Journal* in 1971, he reported that Motorists Mutual was tearing down the front section of its building and erecting a building twenty-one stories tall: "Connected with the expansion will be a restaurant, large, attractive, open-to-the-public and at street level on the northwest corner of Oak Street and Washington Avenue. Above the restaurant will be a parking garage, and all Motorists Mutual buildings on that site will be connected by covered walkways. The architects are Brubaker & Brandt, and Turner Construction Company will put up the structures."

Those structures are still there decades later. The attractive Fire Mark atrium bar and colonial-style dining room was a popular spot for Columbus diners. The venue featured Ohio and Shaker/Amish cuisine. Mark Brackney informed Christine of his former Fire Mark menu favorites: peanut soup and Shaker beef plate, with potatoes surrounding the beef.

Firemark Inn ad. *Courtesy Doug Motz.*

Brackney also explained the meaning of the name Fire Mark and why it was appropriate for an insurance company. A fire mark was put on buildings as a sign that it was protected by a specific fire department. It was a cast-iron plaque proudly displayed. The plaques were painted with the insignia of a fire department, and you could buy replicas of them in the Motorists Mutual gift shop. Apparently, these replicas can still be found at places like the Cracker Barrel.

The Fire Mark was built to look out on the Topiary Park. Motorists Mutual was key in starting the park, much loved for its topiary of Georges Seurat's *La Grande Jatte*, and Motorists Mutual remains a primary sponsor of the park. Soon, a parking lot across from the Fire Mark site will become downtown apartments overlooking the park.

At this writing, the former site of the Fire Mark is home to Plaza Dining and Cafeteria (opened in 1994), a mostly in-house restaurant and catering service, though it is open to the public.

Chapter 4
LAVISH DINING

Ziggy's Continental

1978–1989
3140 Riverside Drive, Columbus

Siegbert Allespach was instrumental in upgrading chef training in Columbus. He also owned the first Columbus restaurant to earn four stars from the *Mobil Guide* (now known as the *Forbes Travel Guide*) in the years 1982 to 1989.

"Ziggy," as he was known, was born in Waldberg, Germany, in 1940. At fourteen, he started his apprenticeship as a chef. In 1960, he began his professional career, cooking in several five-star Swiss hotels. In 1965, he immigrated to the United States to work in Texas at the Dallas–Fort Worth Green Oaks Inn. In 1972, he came to Columbus as executive chef at the Compass Points Restaurant at the Sheraton Hotel, then downtown at 50 North Third Street. Six years later, he opened Ziggy's Continental. His wife, Renate Allespach, trained in hotel restaurant management and service, was always the gracious hostess at Ziggy's Continental.

Martha Johnson Miller remembers that you had to tell the wait staff at Ziggy's at the top of the meal if you wanted a Grand Marnier dessert soufflé, as it had to be made with exact timing. She remembers the "white linen" tablecloths and excellent service for the special occasion that brought one to Ziggy's. Allespach was an early proponent of local food sourcing and the quality of the dining experience.

With Hartmut Handke and Hubert Siefert, Allespach was key in changing the curriculum at Columbus State Community College in the hospitality management program from traditional classroom teaching to European-style apprenticeship training. Students graduate with an associate's degree and are certified sous chefs. Allespach instituted the Columbus chapter of the American Culinary Federation and worked with local chefs to take on apprentices. The first graduates of this program completed in 1980. We have many local chefs who came through this program and/or teach in this continuing program.

Allespach competed in the American and European Culinary Olympics, often winning first, second or third. In Frankfurt in 1976, he won the Gold Medal. Mayor Dana Rinehart declared April 29, 1985, "Ziggy Day."

Ziggy sold his restaurant in 1989 to become executive chef of the Lakes Golf and Country Club, north of Westerville. He was also the chef at the Athletic Club for a time.

Tragically, Allespach drowned, falling through ice in a pond near his home in Powell in February 2014, trying to rescue his dog. He was seventy-four. A dinner to honor Allespach was held at the Refectory to raise money for a room at Columbus State named after Ziggy and his wife.

Today, Gallo's Kitchen & Bar is in a strip mall formerly owned by Ziggy. A Ziggy's menu is hung in a place of honor at the end of the bar. The Watteau drawing, calligraphy and menu items written in French speak volumes about the elegance of Ziggy's Continental. As of this writing, the former Ziggy's restaurant space on Riverside Drive is unoccupied.

THE MEADOWBROOK INN

1947–1960

4785 EAST BROAD STREET, COLUMBUS

Johnnie Flesch (no relation to Mike Flesch of the Grandview Inn) and his wife, Charity, opened an eastside restaurant that attracted quite a bit of notice due to their attention to detail. The building was constructed during World War II, when it was hard to get building materials. That is why the windows were of different sizes.

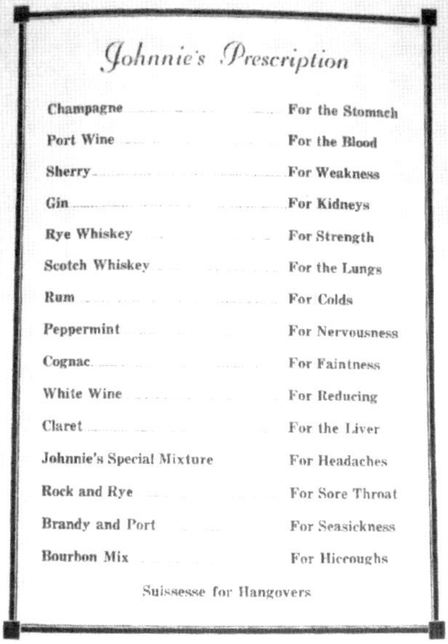

Johnnie's Prescription

Champagne	For the Stomach
Port Wine	For the Blood
Sherry	For Weakness
Gin	For Kidneys
Rye Whiskey	For Strength
Scotch Whiskey	For the Lungs
Rum	For Colds
Peppermint	For Nervousness
Cognac	For Faintness
White Wine	For Reducing
Claret	For the Liver
Johnnie's Special Mixture	For Headaches
Rock and Rye	For Sore Throat
Brandy and Port	For Seasickness
Bourbon Mix	For Hiccoughs

Suissesse for Hangovers

Meadowbrook Inn drink menu. *Courtesy Linda Vollmer.*

In talking to Johnnie's nephew Augustine M. Cosentino (eighty-five years young at this writing), Christine learned that Augustine and two cousins were asked to work in the restaurant for three years of high school, as the restaurant was so busy. Ann "Sugar" Cupoli Vollmer, Charity's daughter, worked in the hat check/coat room and then was the hostess. George Vollmer (Johnnie's son-in-law) worked as a busboy, as did his friends. His sister's future husband, Chuck Krouse, was one of those busboys. "Sugar" and her future husband met at the Meadowbrook.

In addition to relatives, there were "all lady cooks" and, in the dining room, "all waitresses." Flesch selected his meat, chicken and fish personally so that every detail was to his liking. Cosentino and his cousins prepared the cuts of beef, chicken and fish before the dinner business. They also prepared the fresh produce daily. Christine was at the restaurant as a child and remembers Mr. and Mrs. Flesch. She especially remembers the delicious spumoni and tortoni for dessert. Linda Vollmer remembers her grandfather Johnnie making Shirley Temple cocktails for her and her two siblings, John and Ann.

The Meadowbrook Inn did not feature music, as the Flesches wanted to concentrate on the food. They did not want customers who came for drinks and music only. Cosentino, an Aquinas graduate, reports that Governors DiSalle and Lausche frequented the restaurant, along with Edgar P. Wolfe of the *Dispatch* and a group of automobile dealers: Rosenfeld of Chevrolet, Jack Smith of Oldsmobile and Don Cole of Cadillac.

But this popular venue did not continue past 1960. "The recession of the late 1950s killed it," says Cosentino. "Also, there was so much competition by then." Cosentino moved on to the Kroger Company and then to working for the State of Ohio for thirty years. He knew how hard the restaurant business could be from the tender age of fifteen. His uncle retired after the Meadowbrook. His grandson John reports that his grandfather had to have surgery on the tendons of his hands, as he had damaged them cutting meat for so many years.

The site of the Meadowbrook Inn became BancOhio within three months, and then other banks and a Holiday Inn were on the site. At this writing, a Flowerama and the Ashford Senior Community are on the site.

DEL MATTO'S CUCINA ITALIANA

1931–1960
NORTHWEST BOULEVARD AT FIFTH AVENUE AS DEL RIO'S GRANDVIEW

1960–2005
4882 EAST MAIN STREET, COLUMBUS

This restaurant was originally opened by Santo del Matto in Grandview as the Del Rio. The Italian eatery and jazz club, which featured the likes of Dean Martin and Mel Torme, moved to Whitehall in 1960 after a fire destroyed the original. When the restaurant moved, Santo del Matto Jr. took over ownership. The place served Italian food, steaks and chops and featured organ music, as many places of the era did.

Rumors circulated in 1990 that McDonald's or United Dairy farmers wanted to buy the place, but nothing ever came of this talk.

The popular eastside destination was known for its special twenty-ounce lobster dinners, and in 1997, it had two hundred of the crustaceans flown in for a special promotion. It was the kind of place that could support a

Left: Del Matto's neon sign. *Courtesy Mark Del Matto.*

Right: Del Matto's ad. *Courtesy Doug Motz.*

waitress like Charlene Rarey for forty years, beginning her run as a server there in 1962.

In 2003, the restaurant passed again to Santo's son Craig del Matto, who shuttered the popular dining spot in 2005. The building was torn down, and as of this writing, a medical complex occupies the location.

Chapter 5

THEMED RESTAURANTS

The Grandview Inn

1938–1998
1127 Dublin Road, Grandview

The Grandview Inn opened in the late 1930s in an old two-story house with a chunky rectangle added to one side. The chrome furniture and bar fixtures were touted on the grand opening flyer, as were the steaks, chicken and frog legs. The "Dinner Club Room" also had "intoxicating liquors," except on Sundays. There was no mention of the intoxicating jazz that was soon to become the trademark for the lively Grandview Inn.

Mike and Jane Flesch owned the venue for forty years. Later owners were Ollie Rosetti (1978) and B.G. Salvi (1995). Wilhelmina Bookman Orndorff was the chef in the 1950s and '60s. A fire in 1951 destroyed one-third of the building; that section was rebuilt. The Grandview Inn burned completely in 1953. The beautiful brick building was erected in its place, along with the large room with stage.

Jim Loeffler, a jazz historian, remembers the "little bar and lounge" and the array of musicians: Hank Harding; Village Stompers; Jack Teagarden; Count Basie; Terry Waldo; Jimmy McPartland and his wife, Marian Page McPartland; Pee Wee Erwin; Bobby Hackett; and Billy Maxted. When Jim came out of the air force in the mid-1950s, his father took him to the

Above, left: Grandview Inn grand opening. *Courtesy Christine Hayes.*

Above, right: Grandview Inn ad. *Courtesy Doug Motz.*

Below: Grandview Inn lobster Americano. *Courtesy Christine Hayes.*

LOBSTER AMERICANO

1½ to 2-pound live lobster
3 tablespoons butter
1 cup sherry wine
5 ounces celery, chopped
5 ounces carrots, chopped
3 ounces chives, chopped
1 No. 2 can tomato purée
½ lemon, juice
Salt and pepper, to taste

Take live lobster and cut through shell into pieces 1 inch in length. Sauté in butter for 5 minutes. Add 1 cup wine and simmer 10 minutes. Add vegetables, tomato purée and lemon. Season and cook for 15 minutes with lid on skillet. Serves 4.

PAINTING BY ROBERT O'MEARA

Grandview Inn

The address is 1127 Dublin Road (U.S. Highway 33) in Columbus, Ohio. Lunch and dinner served every day except Sunday. M. J. Flesch owns and manages the restaurant. No reservations necessary. Lobster Americano is only one of the many delicious seafood dishes served here. The Grandview Inn is also noted for its charcoal-broiled steaks.

Grandview Inn to see Count Basie: "We had seats next to the piano, and all night I was looking straight into Count Basie's eyes."

Jim was a member of the Central Ohio Hot Jazz Society, and this organization had events over the years at the Grandview Inn. One 1996 event featured Columbus's own Terry Waldo and his Gut Bucket Synchopaters. Terry Waldo now performs and lives in New York City but returns to Columbus each year on his November birthday and performs at Becky's Bungalow.

Three (now highly collectible) record albums were recorded at the Grandview Inn. *Pee Wee Erwin at the Grandview Inn* features a compelling cover designed by Ed Ritter: a nighttime portrait of the brick front with inviting lit windows and patrons arriving. This "on the spot" (the notes read) hi-fidelity recording of Dixieland features the Maxted arrangements for Pee Wee, trumpet; Billy Maxted, piano; Tony Spargo, drums and "salty choruses on the kazoo"; Sal Pace, clarinet; Andy Russo, trombone; and Charlie Troeger, bass. The liner notes for this album were written by Columbus historian Bob Thomas and include this statement: "The great Dixieland music contained in this album was captured for posterity at Mike Flesch's famous and beautiful Grandview Inn in Columbus, Ohio. Here during a month-long summer engagement Pee Wee Erwin and his veteran group recorded this inspired session under the remarkable acoustical conditions afforded the Grandview's smart Longbow Room."

The second album recorded at the Grandview Inn was a posthumous tribute to Bobby Hackett (1915–1976). Oddly, no member of his quartet is attributed, but the notes on the sparse plain blue-and-white cover say the evening was recorded on May 5, 1958.

The third album recorded was *The Big Swingers: Billy Maxted Salutes "The Golden Bear."* Jack Nicklaus and Billy Maxted are seen on the cover in golf shirts and caps on the grass, with Billy at the piano and Jack in full swing with his club in his hand and his golf bag leaning against the piano. In the background is a sand trap. The liner notes are not attributed to anyone. The lineup of the "Manhattan Jazz Band" is Billy, piano; John Dengler, bass sax, trumpet, tuba; Lee Gifford, trombone; Don MacLean, drums; Dan Tracey, clarinet, tenor sax; Ben Ventura, trumpet; and Jack Lesberg, bass.

Jim Loeffler says that in later years at the Grandview, the "feeling changed." In the last years of the Flesch ownership, there was employee theft and several armed robberies, including one in which the Flesches were tied up in the office bathroom. Yet Ben Hayes reports in a column from February 1971, "Mike Flesch has returned from Ft. Lauderdale in time for the sold-out performances of Pete Fountain Friday night in his Grandview Inn—and, while in Florida, booked much more entertainment. Set for the return to the Grandview this year are Woody Woodbury, Four Saints, Mark and Clark, Rhodes Brothers, Stan Kenton, Les Brown, Harry James, Count Basie, and Billy Maxted." Maxted was a favorite of Coach Woody Hayes, and when the coach was not at the Jai Lai, he was at the Grandview Inn to catch a set of Maxted's jazz.

Beyond the Grandview Inn years, the building became a church for a short time and then was torn down in 2001 to make way for a Tim Horton's, which is still on the site.

The Desert Inn

1952–1981
3540 East Broad Street, Columbus

The Desert Inn was a place of exotica in the east end of Columbus. It was owned by the Alexander family: Joe, Albert and Guido. The family had also owned the Palm Garden Night Club on North High Street, where such entertainers as Nat King Cole, Tony Bennett and Dean Martin appeared.

The Desert Inn started out small, but an addition was built later that included the Aztec Room, with the alligator clock and llama skins on the wall. An outdoor pool was built also, with portholes in the side. Under the dining room was the Badlands Bar, from which patrons could see into the pool through the portholes. The female wait staff in the Badlands Bar wore western motif costumes.

In the early 1960s, a great expansion of the venue was undertaken. Maria Alexander, a member of the family, remembers it was "an acre under one roof, with nine or ten party rooms and three full-size kitchens." A motel was planned but never built. The restaurant business was doing well, as the Desert Inn received the overflow from the Kahiki across the street when the Kahiki became too crowded.

Felix Pedon, eighty-five years young at Christine's 2017 interview, was the maître d' in the Aztec Room from the 1950s until 1968. He was a cousin of the Alexanders. Felix remembers the Kenley Players came for dinner or afterhours on Wednesday nights. The Desert Inn featured an Italian menu, porterhouse steak on a sizzling platter and chateaubriand with decorative

Desert Inn ads. *Courtesy Doug Motz.*

potatoes served on a board. Tableside service for Caesar salad and other items was a favorite in the dining room.

Maria Alexander says the entertainment started out with the "mambo people" and "Laugh-In style plays," but the entertainment became too expensive. The Interstate 70-71 development bypassed the east side, while venues on the north side of Columbus prospered, and maintenance of the huge structure was daunting.

The Desert Inn became the Playboy Club. "They put a million dollars into the restoration before they opened," says Maria. At this writing, it is the site of a McDonald's.

Victoria Station

1970s

1691 East Dublin-Granville Road, Linworth

At one time, there were one hundred Victoria Stations in the United States and Canada. In 1986, the company declared bankruptcy. The last one was

Top: Victoria Station ads. *Courtesy Doug Motz.*

Bottom: Victoria Station postcard. *Courtesy CML.*

in Salem, Massachusetts, in 2012, but it was not affiliated with the original company.

The first one was in San Francisco. The model that was copied throughout was made up of American railway boxcars and a caboose, but with décor of antique British railway artifacts. On the "entry platform" was a typical London-style phone booth. The menu included prime rib, steaks, ribs and "Shrimp Victoria" scampi style. The Universal City location was once one of the highest-grossing restaurants in the United States, and Johnny Cash—the man in black—was once even the restaurant's spokesperson!

The layout was always the same: four dining rooms in so many boxcars, seating 125 diners; a cocktail lounge caboose; a bar and waiting room and kitchen on another level. Victoria Stations did promotions for leading sports figures called the "Wiseman Trophy." They kept raising their meal prices, opening more and more Victoria Stations, and the management had seventies-style expensive summit meetings, so they just over-extended themselves. On top of that, they had a competitor at their heels called Railhead Restaurants that was taking on their territories until it was the end of the line for Victoria Station.

As of this writing, the site in Linworth is a farm market.

The Ellis Bakery/Disque/The R&W Bakery

1944–1978

1454 West Fifth Avenue, Columbus

Merwin "Beanie" Bean's career in the Columbus baking business weaves a mighty thread through four famous Columbus institutions. He began working at Foerster's, the 120-year confectionery, bakery and restaurant. (It was not that old when he worked there.) He met his future wife, Iva, because she came to breakfast at Foerster's.

During World War II, Bean worked as a baker for the Curtiss-Wright factory in Columbus. He was transferred and had his family in Los Angeles for the rest of the war.

Back in Columbus in 1947, Bean went to work as the baker in the first Jai Lai on North High Street. He developed the bakery for the new, vast Jai Lai on Olentangy River Road. Christine interviewed his daughter, Sandy Bean Lynch, for this article. Sandy remembers talking to the workers on the steel girders for the new Jai Lai in the early 1950s. She walked out on the girders as a fearless child while she and her father were visiting the building site and nearly stopped her father's heart.

Bean lived on to run the new Jai Lai bakery for two years. This was not a small job; with the huge dining rooms and banquet rooms, the Jai Lai could serve over one thousand people at a time. Bean brought his own recipes to each of the bakeries he worked in. According to his daughter, he had worked as a baker since the age of nine in his hometown of Guysville, Ohio, in Athens County. "Beanie" was known for his pies and his "cakes that could float." Even though he was later divorced from his wife, "he brought us good things constantly," said Sandy.

The fourth Columbus institution is the one he took over, the little bakery at 1454 West Fifth Avenue. Bean was the silent partner. The bakery was called the Ellis Bakery and then went on to be called Disque. Sandy remembers making icing roses for her dad. "I bet I've made ten thousand roses. He used to pay me a nickel apiece for them, and my roses were beautiful."

Later, the bakery was taken over by Ralph Frame and Wilson Gartner and called the R&W Bakery.

The French Loaf

1978–2015

1454–1456 West Fifth Avenue, Columbus

The era of Dave Girves's Jai Lai (this, again, was the second Jai Lai location; the one with the girders) spawned the next bakery in the 1454 Fifth Avenue site. His brother Jim and Ed Kromko were inspired by the Acme Bakery in Berkeley; they noticed people would spend a little more money for quality baked goods. They were also inspired by the Vie de France French bread carts they saw in Los Angeles in 1976. Ed was in engineering, and Jim was in genetics, but they moved back to Columbus and began studying Julia Child's eight- to twelve-page recipe for French bread. They rented space from 1977 to 1978 from Dave Girves at the Jai Lai and began wholesaling French bread. Then they mastered carrot cakes from the recipe of a friend. A 1970s issue of *Bon Appetit* inspired their next triumph: New York cheesecake. The two bakers wholesaled these to restaurants and then took over the R&W, plus the store next door (1456), to create the French Loaf Bakery and sell directly to the public.

All baked goods were fabricated from scratch. Their croissants became famous; they had six varieties filled with differing jams and varieties of Danish, including the cheese Danish. They kept the business from 1978 until 1996, when they sold the thriving venue to Christine and Mark Hawthorne. The Hawthornes sold it, in turn, to a pair of bakers named Mike and Amadeo, who, in turn, sold it to a man named Steve.

At this time, the next-door space was to become a Walgreen's, and the French Loaf was asked to give up a good deal of its baking area. The French Loaf had also become a restaurant, with soups, sandwiches, quiche and other delicacies, in addition to the French baked goods, cakes and cookies.

An off-site space had to be created to bake the goods, and a transport system had to be set up. After a time, Steve sold to Maryjon Lococo, who kept it alive until 2015, when it suddenly closed. A long time passed for the space to be remodeled into the second Si Señor Peruvian sandwich shop in Columbus. The last thing to be changed was the overhead sign, as though the French Loaf was reluctant to leave the area. At this writing, the Si Señor shop has been open just a few months.

FISHERMAN'S WHARF SEAFOOD HOUSE PIER III

1976–1995
1084 MORSE ROAD, COLUMBUS

1997–2005
2143 EAST MAIN STREET, BEXLEY

2011–2014
1611 POLARIS PARKWAY, COLUMBUS

Owners Nick, Niki, Constantin and Bill Chalkias already had two successful seafood restaurants in Cleveland before opening up Fisherman's Wharf Seafood House Pier III in Columbus. "People from Columbus visited our Cleveland restaurants and kept telling us that Columbus needed a good fish and seafood restaurant," said brother Niki in a May 1977 interview with the *Columbus Dispatch.*

Left: Newspaper photo of Fisherman's Wharf. *Courtesy CML.*

Below: Fisherman's Wharf ad. *Courtesy Doug Motz.*

Fisherman's Wharf and Del Matto's ads. *Courtesy Doug Motz.*

When the place opened, more than forty members of the Chalkias family worked in the three restaurants, including five brothers from the Konstantinidis side of the family.

All the food was prepared to order and included a wide range of fish and seafood, including Dover sole, crab and langostinos (giant South American prawns, delicately seasoned, breaded and broiled).

The restaurant quickly became known as two kinds of places: an upstairs area that had delicious food served in a lovely setting and a very posh downstairs area called the Gourmet Room. Its walls were covered with red-flocked wallpaper, the servers wore tuxedos and white gloves and it was outlandishly formal for its time. It isn't hard to imagine how people equated it with an upscale restaurant, as the second stand-alone Clarmont had previously been at the space but only lasted a scant nine months.

Even with all the formality in place, some of the customers' favorites had very humble beginnings. The Fisherman's Special was a thick soup of ground fish and vegetables with a blend of spices from an original recipe of the brothers' mother. Even though a great deal of the recipes initially came from her, the brothers left their hometown in Greece and received restaurant training in Europe, Bermuda and Canada before settling in Ohio. The brothers credited their early successes to their parents' "strong guidance from our father and the prayers from our mother."

The business was so successful that by 1985, "Captain Niki," as Niki came to be known, opened up a deli next door aptly called Niki's Deli. The place piped in Greek music, had a Greek decorative theme and offered typical deli fare such as sub sandwiches and soups, along with Greek dishes and pastries such as gyros, katiafi, baklava and galaktoboureko (small stuffed custard pies).

One of the brothers, Niki, sold his share to the others in 1990 and returned to Greece.

An early fixture of Fisherman's Wharf was "Captain Mike" Reppas, who presided over the Gourmet Room from 1976 to 1993. For a time, he was captain at the Deshler Hotel and then moved to assisting the Chalkias brothers at Pier III. He reportedly danced with the queen of Greece at age seventeen and, while working at the Deshler, waited on the likes of Bob Hope, Milton Berle, Phyllis Diller, Zsa Zsa Gabor and Richard Nixon.

During one memorable evening, the executives at White Castle gathered at the Deshler to celebrate the first drive-through window going up. Reppas recalled, "They all had ordered appetizers, so I sent one of the kitchen boys down the street to pick up forty-four White Castle hamburgers. We dressed them up and served them as White Castles à la Gourmet." This was exactly how the "appetizers" appeared on the bill—at three dollars apiece.

With his retirement in 1993, Captain Mike got out just in time, as Pier III closed its doors in July 1995.

But the Wharf had a comeback in 1997, as Captain Niki, who had returned to Columbus, took over the former Touchstone Café in Bexley to open up Fisherman's Wharf at that location. With this iteration, the kitchen was opened up and the fresh seafood was expanded upon, meaning that the Dover sole would likely have been in the waters off of France just thirty-six hours before being served. The bar at the restaurant was done in a completely nautical theme, bedecked to look like the bow of a fishing trawler.

Fisherman's Wharf ad. *Courtesy Doug Motz.*

It was a true family affair again, as Captain Niki's wife prepared the desserts, son John presided over the bar and daughter Maria was hostess. Niki himself played the butcher of the operation. Additionally, he checked every dish before it was served to make certain that presentation was in order. He even garnished many of the dishes himself.

The success of the reborn Fisherman's Wharf allowed Niki and his business partner, Khaled Ballouz, to take on an additional restaurant at the former Fifty-Five Group restaurant space once housing Café 55. This one was called Wharf II, run by two new partners, Mohammed Khaloug and David Kirk. They decorated the new placc in a nautical theme up and downstairs. The emphasis, as with Fisherman's Wharf, was on seafood. However, it did not last long and, citing a partners' dispute, closed in early 2004.

Not long after Wharf II closed, Captain Niki shuttered the doors on the Bexley locale in the summer of 2005, blaming its closing on construction along Bexley's Main Street.

But ever the phoenix, he rose again and resurrected the Fishinger Road space as the Big Fat Greek Cusina in 2006, featuring Greek delicacies. He also opened up Fisherman's Wharf one last time in 2011 at 1611 Polaris Parkway. It lasted until 2014 and, as of this writing, is a Bar Louie.

Chapter 6

CHAINS

The Kanatas Empire

Troy Restaurant

1947–1956
State and Fourth Street, Columbus

Chef's House and Casa Bonita

about two years each
both on Main Street, Columbus

Don's Drive-In

1955–1980
5500 North High Street, Worthington

Don's Champ Drive-In

1957–1969
1999 South Champion Avenue, Columbus

Don's Briarcliff Drive-In

1958–1985
6998 EAST MAIN STREET, REYNOLDSBURG

Mike Kanatas worked at the AIU Grill (which existed from 1937 to 1954 as a street-front diner in what is now the Leveque) and the QCB in downtown Columbus, where his cooking skills became legend. After World War II, he started the Troy Restaurant with his younger brother Pat. The Troy was popular with politicians, businessmen and people working or visiting at Grant Hospital.

Their brother Tom worked at the Ideal Restaurant and also went into partnership with the widow of the owner of the Chef's House at Eighteenth and Main, circa 1945. At the Ideal, Tom worked twelve hours a day and was paid ten dollars a week. Tom Kanatas also purchased the Casa Bonita on East Main Street and ran it for a few years. He liked it because it was attached to a movie theater. The Troy and the Casa Bonita were sold when the brothers bought Don's in Worthington and, two years later, the Champ, on the corner of Champion and Marion Avenue, just east of downtown and south of Broad Street.

Don's Briarcliff Drive-In. *Courtesy Kanatas family.*

In 1955, the three brothers purchased together the existing drive-in north of Columbus at the gateway to the suburb of Worthington, named "Don's," though this was not any of their names; they kept the name and added it to all their other venues. Don's was a long building with stools at a counter and an awning circling the perimeter of the roof. KANBRO was their corporation, and their work ethic and community spirit became as much the stuff of legend as their cooking.

In 1958, they leased property and built Don's Briarcliff in Reynoldsburg at the corner of Main and Briarcliff. Near to one side was a fire station; many of the drive-in's bottomless thermoses of coffee and delicious doughnuts went

Don's Drive-In, Worthington. *Courtesy Kanatas family.*

there. (Any customer could get a thermos full of coffee for the price of one cup—a Briarcliff feature.) On the other side was a putt-putt miniature golf course. Many people remember ordering Don's food from a speaker at the eighteenth hole of putt-putt, located at a small table and chairs.

Suzanne Kanatas Mardas was the hostess at the Don's Briarcliff opening and remembers that a radio station broadcast live from the restaurant that day.

Don's Briarcliff was well known by truckers and travelers on busy Route 40 (Main Street), as the drive-in was open twenty-four hours a day. Motels proliferated in this section of town; it was the heyday of "see the USA" in the car of your choice. For locals, this was also the kind of place where "everybody knew your name." The Optimists met there, Reynoldsburg City Council met there, friendships were built there. JoAnn Davidson started her political career there; she later became Ohio's first female Speaker of the House. Retirees in Reynoldsburg had a long table that held fourteen people. It was always full of regulars. Some ate all three meals per day there.

John Glenn's parents always stopped by Don's Briarcliff when they drove from New Concord to Columbus. Fortunately for us, this was documented by a photograph in Doral Chenoweth's *Little Weekly*, a Reynoldsburg newspaper.

But where did these three dynamic brothers come from, and why did they land in Columbus? Both their parents immigrated to the United States from Tripoli in Greece to East Moline, Illinois. Two boys were sent—each at age ten, in turn—to work for their bachelor uncle George in Jim Cannell's Quality Bakery in Franklinton (Tom Kanatas in 1923 and Mike in 1926). Both Mike and Tom were driving the delivery truck at age twelve or thirteen. Their younger brother Pat Kanatas also worked at Cannell's Bakery when he came of age. Throughout their lives, they had a camaraderie in their business dealings. They all had to agree. They were approached by franchises, but they kept their restaurants in the family. They had been helped by the Greek community, and they, in turn, helped many Greeks, and indeed anyone in need, all their lives. And they used operating capital, as they hated to ever get in debt.

In 1931, the entire family came to Columbus from Illinois: parents, paternal grandmother, three more brothers, two sisters and two uncles.

During World War II, Mike enlisted and became a cook and then a mess sergeant. He served from Fort Knox to the European theater of war. When

Don's Briarcliff interior, Mike Kanatas greeting customers. *Courtesy Kanatas family.*

Right: Mike Kanatas at Don's Briarcliff. *Courtesy Kanatas family*.

Below: Mr. and Mrs. John Glenn Sr. and Mike Kanatas. *Courtesy Kanatas family*.

Greek American boys were drafted, Mike recommended they be put in military cook school rather than be at the front. He learned to think on a grand scale.

Mike, Pat and their brother Chris Kanatas all enlisted in the army in World War II. Chris was killed in action at Aachen, Germany, in 1944, with General Patton's troops, leaving behind a young wife and a newborn baby girl. The brothers always displayed the flag in their establishments to honor their fallen brother and all the troops. Pete Kanatas tried to enlist but was found to be blind in one eye; Tom was deferred because he became the foreman in the machine shop at Curtiss-Wright. His shop made landing gear for bombers. Tom led blood drives and ran such an efficient shop that he earned medals and commendations. After the war, Tom refused an offer to work for Boeing because he would have to move to Seattle. He chose instead to remain with family in the restaurant business.

The brothers freely shared their knowledge, work ethic, recipes and good humor. After the war, when they had control of their empire, they bailed employees out of jail and lent them money, helped soldiers with PTSD, gave talks to students and became honorary captains of the football team. The family has a copy of a letter from the Brookside Baptist Church saying of the Kanatas brothers, "You will never know what they did for us."

They also loved the fact that their three restaurants spanned the Columbus gateways: the first and last restaurant in each end of town, for travelers on the busy Routes 40 and 23, and Champ's near the Route 33 traffic area. They did not locate a venue in the West End because their friend George had a restaurant there and they did not want to compete with him.

Karen Kanatas Park gave some recollections of her parents, Petro "Pat" and Sara (called Sally), who spent most of their time with the Don's Worthington operation. Her brothers Matthew and Chris both worked there, too, while the sisters, Karen and Lorraine, stayed home and did all the housework and laundry. There was a longtime employee named Glenna who took a bus from Thurman Avenue. Her son Bob also worked there. Don's grilled to order steak, hamburgers and eggs and fried foods such as chicken, fish, pork tenderloins and, of course, French fries, home fries and onion rings. There was chili and breakfast, including hotcakes, at all times. The grilled pecan rolls and strawberry pie—fresh strawberries were always used—were destination favorites. Pies of all kinds were specialties of all the Don's locations. And the featured double-decker burger—wow! At Don's, it was called the "Don's Big Deal," and at Briarcliff it was called the "Don Juan."

At Don's, there was a lot next door to which the carhops would go to take orders if there was overflow. The Boy Scouts and DeMolays sold Christmas trees out of the lot at holiday time—another example of the KANBRO goodwill. More celebrity goodwill: racecar driver and eventual Indy 500 winner Bobby Rahal and his car owner, Jim Trueman, the CEO of Truesports, frequently stopped in on their travels.

Pat and Sally were stuck in the drive-in for three days during the blizzard of 1978. The neighbors walked over, and it was packed. Pat and Sally, who had to sleep on the office floor or desk in shifts, provided coffee for the snowplow workers. The food eventually ran out.

Carhops were a feature at all the drive-ins. They brought out the trays with condiments attached. At first there were speakers at the drive-in stalls. Ted Kanatas found a KANBRO speaker proudly displayed by one of his dorm mates when he went off to college at the University of Dayton. Don's Briarcliff had a more expanded menu than the other drive-ins: a prep kitchen was below the dining room, with a walk-in

Tom Kanatas. *Courtesy Kanatas family*.

freezer, large dry storage, butchering area, dough mixers, three banks of ovens and a dumbwaiter to bring items up to the back of the kitchen. They were the first to feature "broasted" chicken (healthier than fried) in Central Ohio. They made their own bread, doughnuts, onion ring dip, dumplings, pies and, yes, of course, those pecan rolls. No wonder they had to add a banquet room and another large dining room onto the side of Don's Briarcliff!

Mary Beth Kanatas remembers working in Don's Briarcliff and cherished the time she was there, as it was quality time she could spend with her father. Cousins/siblings Suzanne, Ted and Lynne also worked at Don's Briarcliff during their summer breaks and holidays. Many tears were shed at the closing of Don's Briarcliff. The land, which had been leased from Ohio National Bank, an entity that promised never to sell out from under KANBRO, did just that. The new landowner did not keep up the property surrounding the building and literally forced them out with demands of ever-increasing rent.

Don's Briarcliff stopped its twenty-four-hour service within a year of Route 70 opening and diverting the traffic away from Main Street. But the brothers retained their twelve-hour shifts of baking and prepping up until the last day of operation, and the place continued to be the heartbeat of the town. Nevertheless, the "Time to Dine" rotating clock/thermometer on the huge sign was razed, along with the beloved building. The Kanatas brothers were in their seventies and had a last fling as grand marshals of the Tomato Festival Parade in Reynoldsburg. A Burger King went up in the Don's Briarcliff space. It is now gone, too, and an urgent care is being constructed on the site as of this writing.

The land under the leased Worthington Don's was also sold and KANBRO did not renew; another landmark on High Street was razed, along with its beckoning neon sign announcing, "It's Fun to Eat Out." The site became home to a Christian bookstore and a Grease Monkey Oil Change and at this writing is a Monroe Muffler, Carmen's Vacuum and auto-detailing business. Don's Champ Drive-In is still standing, at this writing, as Grand Champions Lounge and Pizza.

Many artifacts of the Kanatas restaurant memorabilia can be seen at the Reynoldsburg Historical Society.

BOB MARVIN'S FIRESIDE INN

MID- TO LATE 1970S
1802 HENDERSON AVENUE, COLUMBUS

FLIPPO'S FOOD SHOPPES

1970S
ORCHARD AND HIGH STREETS AND THEN
UNIVERSITY CITY SHOPPING CENTER, COLUMBUS

Marvin Fishman, alias Bob Marvin, alias Flippo, had two and almost three restaurants in Columbus. The last two were not really a "chain," though perhaps they were meant to expand and be a franchise. Flippo made so many personal appearances that the restaurants may have been too much for his schedule. Apparently, he did not like to talk about the restaurants because in the film made by Frank Cromer, *TV Clown*, no mention was made of this phase of Marvin's life.

Bob Marvin was a vocalist and sax player in the early '50s at WBNS Channel 10 in Columbus on a show called *Homemakers Hobnob*, a variety show with Jean Shea and Tom Gleeba as co-hosts. In 1953, Marvin stepped in as the clown host on the *Tip-Top Bandwagon*, a half-hour show with fifteen minutes of cartoons. (The popular Tip Top Gay Street eatery in the former Grapevine café took its name from this show.)

This evolved into *The Early Show* (1963), two hours with an hour of cartoons or *The Little Rascals*. Everyone in Columbus tuned in to see the ridiculous skits and in-jokes. Many local children, and stars passing through town, appeared on the show with Flippo because of their affiliation with one group or another. It was natural for such a beloved figure as Flippo to have his face on a restaurant. Marvin continued as a clown on Channel 10 until 1977.

The Fireside Inn at Reed and Henderson came into being late in Flippo's clown career. It was in the Northwest Shopping Center. Local musicians Jim Loeffler, Dan Emch and David Houser remember it as one big room that was filled with jazz. Another attraction was that after eating at the Fireside, the patrons received free passes to the Loew's Arlington movie house next door during the weekdays. The Fireside was tucked away in a passageway next to the theater (at this writing, the theater is Sears). The club/restaurant

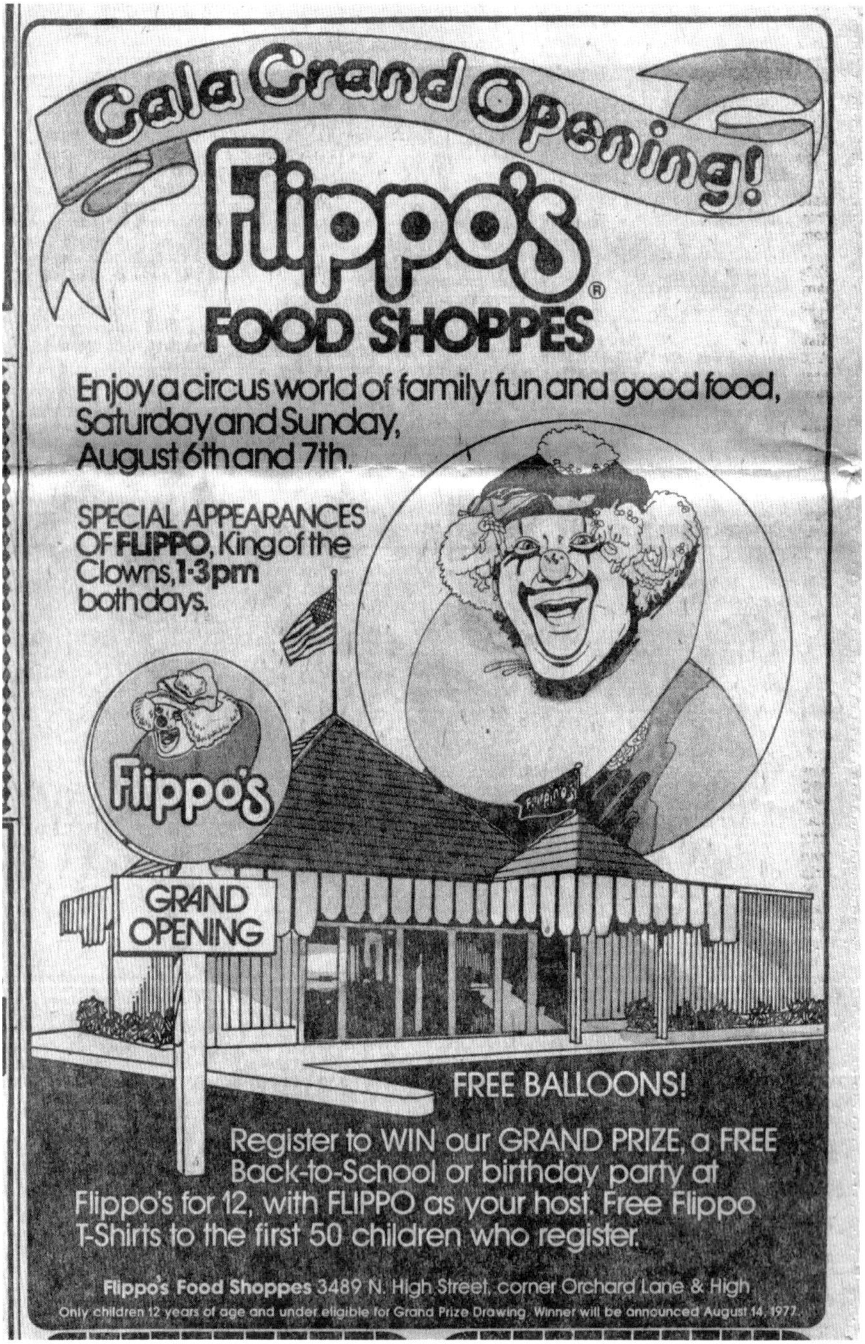

Flippo's Food Shoppes gala grand opening. *Courtesy Christine Hayes.*

featured dancing on weekends. The Fireside was a "money pit" for Marvin, apparently, so he let it go. At this writing, it is the Silla Restaurant.

The second restaurant associated with Bob Marvin is Flippo's Food Shoppes at Orchard and High, with a grand opening in August 1977. This would have also been near the time Marvin's tenure with Channel 10 was waning. Marvin left the television station with the rights to his Flippo persona (and the costume).

Marvin had an office on King Avenue to manage his affairs. He was the spokesperson for an interactive, pay-for-view television station, QUBE. He was a common sight driving around in his customized Isetta. He arrived at the Ohio State Fair in a helicopter, a sight well remembered by those who had never seen the clown up close.

The third restaurant, in the University City shopping center, never opened. Flippo's Ice Cream Factory was to have been the name. In 1983, Marvin retired from the clown biz but still made the occasional personal appearance in the Isetta. He donated his costume to the Ohio History Connection and passed away in 2006.

The site of Flippo's Food Shoppes at Orchard and High Streets is now a Donato's Pizza.

Rigsby's

Cuisine Volatile

1986–2015
698 North High Street, Columbus

K2U

1989–2002
641 North High Street, Columbus

Indigo 88

1989–1990
700 North High Street, Columbus

Flatiron Bar and Diner

1991
129 EAST NATIONWIDE BOULEVARD, COLUMBUS

Café Rigsby

2001–2003
180 MARKET STREET, NEW ALBANY

In writing about Kent Rigsby's landmark Short North Columbus restaurant, we went looking for the best way to describe the thought process that went into creating such a beloved and highly respected eatery. Fortunately, our friend Doral Chenoweth had already done that; these are his words about Rigsby's Cuisine Volatile from the *Columbus Dispatch* printed on September 21, 1986 (it opened on February 20, 1986):

> *This is the story of a 33-year-old dreamer who washed dishes, waited tables, and then waited until the time and tables were right for Columbus to support an outstanding restaurant, one of quality befitting any noted culinary capital in the world. Kent Rigsby is a dour and dark-eyed entrepreneur who creates excitement in a kitchen that becomes living theater in a place for dining. Rigsby trained for the theater, one of his first loves. He planned a restaurant as a playwright would a script. He had the story in his mind; he knew the dialogue for each of his intended characters. He knew blocking and casting when he sat down to paper. He choreographed the dance and music.*
>
> *Then, like any good theater man, he went looking for angels.*
>
> *Long before Rigsby took a curtain call in the Short North—this city's off-Broadway for restaurants—he played out every role in both San Francisco and France, the meccas for dreaming restaurateurs.*
>
> *Rigsby is a hometown boy, the son of Dr. and Mrs. William Rigsby of Upper Arlington. He is a graduate of Columbus Academy and has a theater degree from Ohio Wesleyan University in Delaware. He is a sensitive poet at heart, which probably accounts for his love affair with restaurants.*
>
> *Rigsby's attention turned to two culinary artisans. He talks tenderly of Madeleine Kamman, who learned to cook before attending the Sorbonne and Cordon Bleu cooking schools in Paris. (Kamman now lives in Glen,*

N.H., where she runs a cooking school and writes books.) Rigsby credits the Cuisine Volatile name to her influence and that of world-class Chef Fredy Girardet. Girardet once wrote of "cuisine sponatie." Kamman speaks of "cuisine personnelle."

"I wanted a watchword, something aggressive with flavor. Something volatile...volatile just dropped into place," Rigsby explained.

Then the recipe for Rigsby's Cuisine Volatile fell into place:

1. Be idealistic about food.

2. Innovate with today's culinary cultures.

3. Have an exacting plan for cuisine and equipment.

4. Staff with trained, working culinary professionals.

5. Pull together investors with $420,000, or good lines of credit.

Mix all of the ingredients with one loving and understanding wife/partner. Simmer, stirring constantly, for several months before serving. Spread over a good location. Slice into ample portions for hungry and appreciative patrons. Prepare fresh daily.

Rigsby's plan took form over the months he worked in San Francisco. In the early '80s, he spent 18 months at the California Culinary Academy, but he credits his real kitchen training to the two-plus years he was sous chef to the noted Marcel Cathala at Maurice et Charles in San Rafael, Calif.

Maurice et Charles is a two-chef kitchen, just large enough to make one small turnaround. There Rigsby learned to cut meats in true French fashion. (Growing up on fast food didn't prepare him for cutting out a whole wild boar.) With Cathala, Rigsby curried his talents for sauces and, possibly, the exotics that appear on the Volatile menu, with daily changes.

If he learned his French classics at Maurice et Charles, Rigsby got his summer straw-hat exposure working in the high-volume kitchen of San Francisco's popular "Washbag," the Washington Square Bar & Grill. There, he followed a set list of menu standards that prepared him for his return home.

Rigsby came home in 1983 to be executive chef for Sue Doody's wildly popular Lindey's in German Village. It was never a secret that he would open his own place some day. Doody, the equally popular personality of her own restaurant, encouraged him.

Rigsby quit Lindey's in April 1985 after some two years in that high-volume establishment. After the hectic pace, Rigsby knew one thing for certain: His restaurant had to have an urban location with a major Downtown draw. Hence the Short North, a changing neighborhood to challenge the quaintness of German Village.

Rigsby's ad. *Courtesy Doug Motz.*

Short North developer Sandy Wood had a raw space at 698 North High, and he also had a connection with architect Bob Wandel. Kent and Bob worked to create the design aesthetic, with the south wall exposing raw brick hung with art from the early Short North galleries. The north wall was covered with white ceramic tile that was accented with red squares in a single line that were inspired by something Kent had seen in Italy. The clean, simple white tablecloths were very purposeful, as he didn't want the décor to clash. His desire was for any color in the place to come from the food being served and the diners who came in.

The open-concept kitchen was among the first in Columbus and allowed patrons to see what was happening and to allow Kent to closely monitor preparations.

A sweet early detail came from one of Rigsby's lieutenants, Tom Callaghan. Tom was a graduate of the Culinary Institute of America, and his mother created the bread baskets for Rigsby's—each with a monogrammed "R" in the center.

Early highlights of the menu included sautéed tenderloin of rabbit with eggplant purée in a curry sauce over wild rice and raisins; capellini with fresh tarragon and smoked scallops in a sauce of chopped tomatoes, onions, garlic and white wine and red vinegar; Mediterranean-style grilled lamb chops served with feta and black olives; and farm-raised catfish in a light beer batter.

Kent expected to cater to a yuppie crowd, but he shared that never really happened. He said he really catered early on to folks closer to his parents' age, whom he nicknamed "woppies": wealthy older people.

Some folks early on felt that the Short North needed to drive out some of the rougher element. It's difficult for a reader today to imagine a Short North with drug dealers and prostitutes, but that is part of the landscape that was faced by early pioneers such as Rigsby.

It was important to Kent that his restaurant have local art. He shared, "I really wanted to have some original art. Something representing my own tastes, sort of contemporary and aggressive, like the cuisine here." To that end, he featured the work of John Donnelly, Susan Behrman and even his own father, Dr. William Rigsby. "I didn't choose art that would stay six months and change over. The art is part of the decor."

In 1989, he decided to open up K2U at 641 North High Street. "The food focus will be on seafood," Rigsby said at the time. "Casual seafood—salads, lox and bagels, fried fish sandwiches, oyster sandwiches, lobster and crab rolls. It harkens back to my experience in San Francisco with oyster bars. And I spent some time in England where you can go in a storefront fish and chips place, get a drink and order something to eat. This will be an amalgam of an English fish and chips house and an American oyster bar."

This was funded through solicitations by Kent and RMW I Ltd Partnership, which sought sixteen investors at $10,000 each to augment a $160,000 loan and a $70,000 lease obligation, for a total of $390,000 to be used for equipment leases and furnishings.

K2U did very well for many years. There was live jazz music on Mondays, and a mural painted by Rigsby's father featuring the likenesses of famous musicians, actors and historical notables spanned the room. Food served included *pasta e fagioli*, a staple bean and pasta soup, savory and uncomplicated, flavored subtly with rosemary; and penne *al'arrabbiata*, another simple but delicious vegetarian pasta. It is worth mentioning that K2U had a great bar with a great selection of single-malt scotches, top-shelf bourbons and cordials, such as chartreuse and even honey liqueur. K2U closed its doors in 2002 after Sandy Wood of the Wood companies chose not to renew the lease.

At the same time that Rigsby was opening K2U, he was working to bring back former Columbus city councilman Jerry Hammond's defunct jazz club Major Chord at 700 North High Street. That came to pass, and he opened up the club next door to Rigsby's and renamed it Indigo 88 in November 1989 as a not strictly jazz club that served casual bistro fare. However, the tiny kitchen at the place and the responsibilities from his burgeoning restaurant family combined to spell trouble for the club, which closed in late 1990.

In 1991, Kent was part of the initial group that opened Flatiron Bar and Diner at 129 East Nationwide Boulevard. The place had a trademark marble bar, wooden flooring and a narrow dining room with a black-and-white tiled floor.

Rigsby's added brunch to the menu in 1992 by offering dishes such as buckwheat sourdough pancakes with honey syrup, poached eggs on black bean cakes and fajitas with goat cheese and tomato-onion ragout.

Rigsby's lamb. *Courtesy Doug Motz.*

As a celebration of being described as the best Italian place in Columbus, in the spring of 1994, Sundays at Rigsby's officially became Italian, complete with red-and-white checkered tablecloths and Italian opera playing throughout the place.

In 1998, the mentor became the chef when Chef Marcel-Henri Cochet came from San Francisco to become head chef for Rigsby's. In Cannes, he was chef of the Hotel Martinsee, and in London, he served as chef of the Hotel Berkeley.

Kent and his wife, Tasi Rigsby, decided to try out a country club theme in New Albany in 2001. Tasi said the New Albany restaurant, Café Rigsby, was opened with high expectations and delivered a good product. It specialized in southern French peasant fare, characterized by appetizers such as duck confit. Sadly, the place was unable to develop a strong following and closed in 2003, fourteen months after opening.

In January 2005, Rigsby's took a little time to renovate and moved the bar from the rear of the building to the High Street side. Additionally, seating increased to accommodate 120 patrons.

In 2010, Bethia Woolf's Columbus Food Adventures added Rigsby's to the Short North walking tour, originally consisting of Knead, Le Chocoholique, Tasi Café, Rigsby's and Jeni's Splendid Ice Creams. In 2012, Kent Rigsby was named a finalist for the prestigious James Beard Award for best chef in the Great Lakes region.

But all good things must come to an end, and on Saturday, November 7, 2015, Rigsby's closed its doors. Following is the announcement Kent Rigsby posted on Facebook the following day:

> *The curtain came down for the final time last night, on the long run that was Rigsby's kitchen. I'm saddened by this reality and at the same time proud and grateful for the amazing memories and experiences that come with 29 years of running one of Columbus' top restaurants. Thank you to the wonderful customers who have graced our doors over the years. I have met so many incredible people and developed many life-long friendships. And thank you to so many talented and hardworking people who I have been so fortunate to work with side by side over these many years.*
>
> *And GRAZIE MILLE, (there is just more poetry in the Italian language), but I really feel it, 1000 thanks to all you caring and lovely people that have posted here. Rest assured, I have so much to be thankful for, especially the health of my family and their individual greatness. I look forward with energy and excitement to my next professional challenge. There will soon be a new curtain rising on my next act. I'll keep you posted!*

Rigsby's was a place of many Columbus firsts: the first open kitchen, the first place serving artisanal pizzas, the first place with substantial house-made bread, the first real cheese course and the first place to innovate among the cuisines of the Mediterranean.

As of this writing, Tasi Café, run by Kent's wife, Tasi, is going strong in the Short North, and Kent Rigsby is the chef at the New Albany Country Club.

THE AMES FAMILY

Frezno Eclectic Kitchen

1994–2003
782 NORTH HIGH STREET, COLUMBUS

2013–2014
460 SOUTH FRONT STREET, COLUMBUS

Dagwoodz

1995–2002
660 NORTH HIGH STREET, COLUMBUS

Press Grill

1998–2002
741 North High, Columbus

Café Iliana

2004
150 East Gay Street, Columbus

Cinco

2008–
1 South High Street, Columbus

Café Lola

2008
12 East Broad Street, Columbus

Burgers, Dogs and Fries

2009–2012
12 North High Street and Columbus Commons, Columbus

Jack Whitney's

2013
520 South Front Street, Columbus

After running their Ames-to-Please pushcart business in front of the Rhodes Tower on East Broad Street for several years, Lori and Kevin Ames decided to open up a brick-and-mortar space in the Short North called Frezno in 1994. The place became known for serving terrific pizzas (one of the most popular was a grilled lime chicken with provolone, cheddar, house salsa, guacamole and sour cream) from a wood-burning oven, as well as a solid variety of pasta. Another big draw was Lori Ames's mother, Marlene Mattevi's fried green tomatoes. The secret: frying them in good old-fashioned lard! But Marlene didn't supply just the tomatoes; she supplied all the homemade desserts as well. Also, Chef Jeff Bentley became well known for his inventive menus and for sporting a panama boater while tending to the wood-fired oven.

With Frezno doing well, the couple set their sights on the space occupied by the former Bermuda Onion (often nicknamed the "Nelly Deli") to serve all-day breakfast. This eatery came to be known as Dagwoodz and was one of author Doug Motz's favorite places to eat when he owned the inclusive LGBT-themed bookstore An Open Book. His favorites included chocolate chip pancakes and duck sausage. There was a booth in the back of the place that was his favorite. It was small and had only a bench that faced the front door. It was the perfect place to dive into the Sunday *New York Times* and enjoy some good strong coffee with breakfast while reading the *Times* "Book Review."

As at Frezno, Marlene Mattevi baked all of the delicious cakes that were served, making at least eighteen a week. However, even her terrific baked goods and Doug's Sunday patronage couldn't keep the place open, and they shuttered their doors in 2002. As of this writing, the space is home to the Happy Greek.

The couple had plans to start a Mexican eatery named Caravanz as well as an upscale chop shop that was to be called Carolinaz, but neither of these came to fruition. One venture that did come to fruition was their reopening of the Press Grill at 741 North High in 1998.

But perhaps their expansion was part of the reason for the demise of Frezno in the Short North in the summer of 2003. From 2004 to 2006, the location was home to the well-regarded Zola Café. As of this writing, the former Frezno is home to the wildly popular Union Café, which was initially based on the Los Angeles eatery Abbey Food & Bar.

After selling Frezno, Dagwoodz and Press Grill, Lori and Kevin opened up Café Iliana at 150 East Gay Street. The couple then opened Burgers, Dogs and Fries at Columbus Commons and Café Lola at Broad and High in 2008, followed closely by Cinco in the Huntington Building, offering burritos, tacos and salads.

In 2013, they sold all the restaurants they had to concentrate on a reimagined Frezno in the Brewery District at 460 South Front Street in the former Dom's Fish Market location. "We had been approached by people in the past about selling our many eateries. Once that got into our head, we thought maybe it was the way we wanted to go," Kevin Ames said. "We sold because we knew we couldn't really go into Frezno and not be there all the time. We didn't want other people running it for us. To make this work, we knew we needed to be there every day."

The idea was to take all of their most popular dishes and desserts from the many restaurants they had owned and operated over the years and put all of that under one roof. However, they were offered the opportunity to take over the former Handke's space at 520 South Front, down the street from Frezno's second iteration, and took it. They renamed the place Jack Whitney's, then reopened it as Front Street Bar and Grill, which is now closed.

The Delewese Family

The Delewese family—the name was originally D'Alessandro—came from Pettorano sul Gizio, province of Aquila, in central Italy. Brother Rocco came to America at the age of eleven. Brother Sam came to Columbus in 1912 with his new wife and child to witness the marriage of Rocco to Lucia DeVictor, a native of the same Italian village and sister to their business partner, Guy DeVictor. "Rock" was a superintendent at Marble Cliff Quarries and worked at the Gloria, the family's first

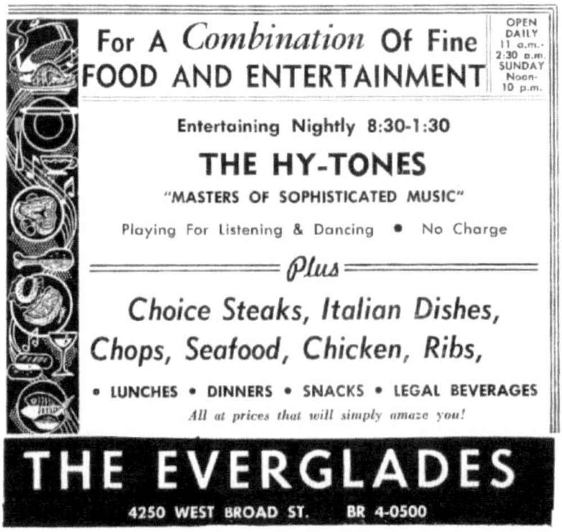

Everglades ad. *Courtesy Doug Motz.*

Left: Everglades. *Courtesy Christine Hayes.*

Below: Everglades ad. *Courtesy Christine Hayes.*

restaurant venture, when needed. Brother Ben owned the Dublin Restaurant; brother Tony owned the Riviera and the Everglades. One assumes all the brothers, cousins, wives and children had a hand in making this Columbus restaurant empire a success. Here are some of the stories.

The Gloria

1925–1993
2195 RIVERSIDE DRIVE, COLUMBUS

Gloria ad. *Courtesy CML.*

Sam and Rocco Delewese, with partner and brother-in-law Guy DeVictor, opened the Gloria Barbecue in 1925 as a small building housing a soda fountain and a nearby outdoor barbecue pit in Upper Arlington at 2195 Riverside Drive. Ham, beef and pork barbecue were cooked on the pit. In 1926, the partners built a dining room for one hundred people, and then in 1928, a dance hall was added with a small stage. The Gloria Barbecue became the Gloria Nightclub. In the early 1930s, another project created the roof garden for dancing under the stars. An elevated floor was provided for bigger shows in the nightclub. The exterior of the restaurant was stone, while that of the nightclub was stucco. Early menus show sandwiches, chicken and steak as the cuisine.

Top acts were featured at the Gloria for decades. The Four Freshmen and Dean Martin and many big bands packed people in. Wedding parties were a specialty for this now Italian food restaurant. Harry Jarkey, a local comedian, was the club's master of ceremonies. The floor show featured singers, dancers, magicians and comedians. Ray and Henry Cincione were regular attractions with their dance bands. In the early '60s, "Twist" contests were featured and Hobby Horse races, in which customers and waitresses took part, provided great fun.

In addition to the club, the Delewese brothers were partners in a grocery in San Margherita. Until he became day manager of the Gloria, Guy DeVictor, who had married Donata Delewese, operated the Delewese Grocery, which was run by Rock's son and daughter, Frank and Lola, in later years.

Many of the Delewese and DeVictor sons and daughters worked at the Gloria over the years. During World War II, while young men were in the service, the nightclub had an "honor roll" for its employees. A plaque hanging above the doorway paid tribute to them, and World War II posters dominated the décor.

Sam Delewese died in 1955. Rocco's sons, Frank (and Frank's wife, Dori, who ran the kitchen) and Aldo, ran the Gloria thereafter. Moving along with the times, the Gloria hosted teen dances, with such bands as the Dantes from Worthington and the Electras before they became the Fifth Order.

In 1970, the Gloria burned to the ground. On the site, the Gloria rose again as an Italian restaurant called the Gloria Lounge and Restaurant, but this time without a nightclub, and an adjacent gas station. The former gas station became the Skyward Grille, owned by Dori Delewese's niece Jennifer Ratliffe and her husband, Mike. At this writing, the building is up for sale, but Skyward exists as a street food vendor at local festivals.

The second Gloria closed on April 3, 1993. At this writing, the site is an El Vaquero Mexican restaurant.

The Beechwold Tavern

1934–1940

4784 North High Street, Clintonville

The Delewese family, owners of already-established Columbus restaurant the Gloria, erected the Mission-style building at 4784 North High Street in Clintonville (this area was then called Beechwold) in 1934. For eight years prior, Tony Delewese had operated the Beechwold Bar-B-Q (4848 North High Street) a few hundred feet north of the new tavern. With its opulent ballrooms and terrazzo flooring, the Beechwold was the local hot spot for parties and dances with live music, especially for fraternities and sororities. Henri Boyd purchased the building in 1940 and renamed it Henri Boyd's Beechwold Restaurant. He featured steaks, chicken and fish.

In 1965, the Golden Bull became the name of the restaurant. Colors of the exterior, prior to this, went from whitish to pinkish. "The Bull" was brownish and featured a cafeteria, a restaurant with servers and party rooms as before.

Subsequently, the building exterior became white again and housed Lindy Productions, a film company; Ohio Newsfilm, a TV news service; Magnetic Studios, a sound recording company; the Reserve, a carpet store; Azia Oriental Rugs; and Cord Camera.

Anand and Doris Saha purchased the thirteen-thousand-square-foot building in 2012 and restored it and its well-worn terrazzo flooring and had the interior newly decorated in Austrian style, as that is the flavor of their culinary fare and elaborate pastries at Mozart's. Five grand pianos embellish as many rooms so music and community feeling and parties can flourish once again in the neighborhood. The exterior color is now a striking Burnt Aztec Red, and an outdoor patio gives diners an option for fresh air.

The Riviera Restaurant and Bar

1936–1954
360 Sandusky Street, Columbus

Tony Delewese's Art Deco Riviera, with its clean lines and parquet glass windows, was at 360 Sandusky Street on the Scioto Peninsula. It was located near the intersections of Sandusky (now Route 315) and Spring Streets, at the confluence of Columbus's two rivers, the Olentangy and the Scioto. It featured a large dining room and bar decorated in black and red. The Gene D'Angelo Band performed nightly at the Riviera before D'Angelo became the general manager of Columbus Channel 10. The Riviera was razed in the making of the Spring/Sandusky Interchange. The Boat House Restaurant now sits near the site of the Riviera.

Capuano Family Restaurants

Cappy's and Sons Deli

1949–2005
103 South High Street, Columbus

Yesteryear Sandwich Shop

1972–1977
Town and High Streets, Columbus

Olde Summit Towne

1973–2012
16143 Broad Street, Pataskala

Big Ten Restaurant

1977–1985
Town and High Streets, Columbus

The dynastic story of the Capuano family begins in Palermo, Sicily, the birthplace of the family's first entrepreneur, Enrico Capuano. Having no real skills and speaking very little English, Enrico came to America in 1912 and settled in the Italian immigrant community of Marble Cliff. The story goes that in order to make a living, he built a wooden pushcart and peddled bananas door to door from a produce supplier he hooked up with. His grandson Chuck Capuano relayed that "he couldn't speak English, so he'd hold his finger up and say, 'One cent, one cent!' He took in twenty dollars his first day out selling bananas a penny apiece. He was so proud of that story."

After saving as many pennies as he could from the banana business, Enrico was able to open a vegetable stand in the old Central Market. (It was located where the Greyhound bus station is located as of this writing.) He drafted his son Severio "Cappy" Capuano to assist him at the market. That's where he introduced Cappy, Chuck's father and the third of eight siblings, to the produce business.

The market is also where Enrico got the nickname the "Celery King." "He would purchase ripening celery and get kids to clean it down to the hearts. My dad would tell me that they would trim so much celery it would be up to their waists," said Chuck.

The Central Market business was good, but Enrico didn't have any formal education, so he didn't really know how to properly keep the shop's books. "When he made a sale, he would write it down with a pencil," Chuck said. "My grandmother was educated, and when he went home at night, she would add it all up."

When Enrico was ready to retire, Severio took over the family business. Fortunately for the family, he inherited every bit of his father's knack for business.

Severio was able to send his son Chuck to college, where he received a degree in industrial design. But the restaurant bug was very much in him as well.

> *OSU placed me as a student to Owens-Illinois on the South End, where I designed packaging for them. I even designed a smart funnel system for them, but they wouldn't pay me for it. They did pay me $10,000 for every patent I got for them, and I was able to save some money.*
>
> *I did pretty well for them, and they ended up sending me to Toledo, where I helped Libbey Glass and came up with three more patents. But my wife didn't like Toledo, so we moved back down to Columbus.*

At that time, Central Market was charging Cappy thirty-five dollars a month for his vegetable stand, and word was out that the market would be coming down. Chuck recalls, "I went to the Neil House and asked what they were going to do with an empty storefront. The manager thought I was crazy when I told him I wanted to sell fruit baskets there. I convinced him to rent me the space during Christmas, and in that month we made $15,000 on fruit baskets! And I was still working for Owens-Illinois."

That money allowed the family to set up shop at 103 South High Street. Chuck recalls:

> *Dad named it Cappy's and Sons Deli. We sold sandwiches and fruit baskets and managed to keep the place going until 2005!*
>
> *Dad and I also opened the Yesteryear Sandwich Shop at Town and High about 1972. We would open at eleven o'clock and sold soup, sandwiches and pastries from our cousin's Italian bakery. The place was set up cafeteria style and continued for four and a half years.*
>
> *Anthony Thomas told my father they were interested in setting up shop at Yesteryear, so my dad sold it to them.*
>
> *The Sabre Lounge was across the street, and the family had a forever lease on the property, as well as a liquor license. We were able to convince the family to sell it to us, and we renamed it the Big Ten. It was decorated with Big Ten pennants and all kinds of college memorabilia.*

The family also had a tenant in a space upstairs who ran a beauty parlor, and next to the building was a wig shop.

Big Ten had terrific lunch specials like roast beef with mashed potatoes, and the hot fudge sundaes were popular with the girls who would come in from St. Joseph's Academy. It also became a big hangout for Lazarus employees.

> *We would sell the Lazarus folks liquor in coffee cups during their work breaks so their supervisors wouldn't know that they were drinking!*
>
> *We had that store from about 1977 to 1985. Biggest mistake we ever made was kicking out our basement tenant. He had a shop that sold adult novelties, and we didn't want that so close by, so we gave him ninety days to vacate. We then brought in a man who sold clothing and shoes to ample-sized ladies. He was always fighting with his wife, and one night he came to the store to sleep after they had a big fight. Apparently, he left a cigarette burning because that night he burned the whole place down! Fortunately, we had insurance and started to look for another place.*

While all of this was going on with the fruit stand, another branch of the Capuano family had heard of a hotel in Pataskala that was going to be coming on the market in 1973. Chuck says, "We heard about it from the president of Buckeye Federal, which was a local downtown banking institution. The family that had owned it had fallen on hard times and were looking to possibly sell."

Chuck and his brother Buddy went in on it together, and since Chuck had the design degree, he transformed it from a hotel to a restaurant and even added a large party room on the back and renamed it Olde Summit Towne, since it was out in Summit Station near Pataskala. Chuck recalls:

> *All of the renovation occurred during the energy crisis, and I had to grow a beard just to stay warm while renovating!*
>
> *During the first year we were open, Western Electric* [6150 East Broad and as of this writing the corporate service center of Mount Carmel Hospital] *had big banquets with us and helped establish us as the go-to banquet space for the far east end of Franklin County and near west side of Licking County.*
>
> *My brother and I were in on this one together, but he had some horses at Beulah Park and I was working really hard at Olde Summit Towne. After a year, I asked him if he would buy me out so I could work on some of our other family places, which he did.*

Chuck then bought the old Sohio Station across the street for parking and also built a drive-through on the lot.

Olde Summit Towne. *Courtesy Doug Motz.*

Buddy and his wife, Kay, went on to run the business very successfully—initially as a full-service eatery and, after two years, as a buffet-style restaurant. Olde Summit Towne could seat up to 540 patrons when all of the party rooms were filled as well as the main dining room. Eventually, the staffing grew to 30 employees and a side business catering for general aviation aircraft operating out of most of Columbus's airports.

But by August 2012, Buddy and Kay were feeling the weight of thirty-nine years at the place, and at seventy-two years old, they decided enough was enough and closed Olde Summit Towne. Coughlin's Automotive bought the place from them for a tidy sum.

When Chuck was bought out by Buddy, he started looking around for another venue and heard about Emil's. Emil Windmiller was looking to sell, and Buddy made him an offer and turned the Steer Inn into Capuano's.

He redecorated with Tiffany lamps, velvet curtains and windows painted with old-fashioned designs. He smartly kept on the from-scratch bakers and their signature desserts.

One day, Frank Benson III came in to Capuano's and told Chuck that the Kroger at Main and Hamilton was going to be for sale, as the Kroger company was building a larger store nearby. Frank was a developer, and Chuck told him he thought the large building would make a terrific disco, and thus Charlie Bear's was born! (The name is Chuck's given name, Charles, coupled with a nickname his wife gave him due to a small potbelly he had at the time.) Chuck remembers, "We opened Charlie Bear's on a night with a level-one snow emergency, and folks were still lining up to get into the place. We just killed it with that place!"

After starting the disco, Chuck sold Capuano's to a dentist. "I hired dancers for the place and was able to pay off Emil the $60,000 I owed him—in cash!" Emil did enjoy coming into Charlie Bear's and could often be found flirting with some of the pretty girls doing the hustle.

This gave Chuck the idea that he could do something even bigger, and when he heard that the discount store Fisher Big Wheel in Lancaster was going out of business and was in bankruptcy proceedings, he took a trip down to look it over. The place was huge, and he ended up leasing it for $6,500 a month. He decided to turn it into a western-themed village and called it the Charlie Horse.

> *We had several shops inside the place that sold everything from purses, old-time photos, clothes and even auto parts. We created a big country music room and a smaller rock-and-roll place. All of the big country stars traveled there, including Hank Williams Jr. I just collected 10 percent off the receipts from all of the shops and did my best to keep big names coming to the country room. That place was so busy, our server had to use shopping carts to carry out all the meals and drink orders!*
>
> *We were only open there four nights a week and doing great until the City of Lancaster decided to buy the property and we had to close it. The Charlie Horse lasted four and a half years.*

Chuck's son was attending Wittenberg in Springfield, and he heard of a place that was for sale. Chuck opened up Charlie Stars with a similar concept to the Charlie Horse but on a much smaller scale. His manager really wanted to buy into the business, but Chuck wasn't interested in selling to him. The manager was disgruntled and burned the place down. Chuck ended up selling the property to a church.

He then bought a place at Third and King Avenues and called it B Hampton's. His daughter Cathy Capuano ran it for fifteen years.

Today, the family has Bullwinkle's on campus, and Chuck told us it had a lot of items that were used in Charlie Bear's.

As of this writing, Chuck is semi-retired and living in Buckeye Lake. When Doug asked if he had any memorabilia from his places, he told him, "I sure did—three big boxes that I just threw away!" This is a man who lives in the now, but wow, would we have loved to have seen what treasures were in those boxes!

Chapter 7
FARTHER AFIELD

Bellefontaine

Bellefontaine has the highest point in Ohio, Campbell Hill, within its city limits. In 1777, it was the site of Blue Jacket's Town, where the Shawnee war chief had his main encampment. It was a main terminal for railroads beginning in the 1890s. Bellefontaine has the first street in the United States to be paved with concrete.

Shiveley's

1957–1965
1117–1119 South Main Street

Even though this iconic restaurant lasted but a short time, it was the Logan County equivalent of the *American Graffiti* experience for Bellefontaine teens, complete with carhops in uniform with trays that fastened on car windows. Pizza ("Hearth-Baked") was the specialty, but burgers, fries and milkshakes were also legendary. The inviting art-deco sign and waving flags beckoned the customers in. The rise and demise of this wonderful haven must have been like a door on another world opening and then sadly shutting.

Bellville

Bellville, founded in 1808, once was part of a gold rush on Dead Man's Run. The village downtown prides itself on its "Norman Rockwell" look.

Banks' Soda Grill, later the San-Dar Smorgasbord

1948–1994
96 Main Street

In 1948, Dorothy and Eugene Banks opened Banks' Soda Grill, a small place that could hold twenty-six people. This place had hamburgers and short-order items, in addition to soda drinks. A dining room was added in 1950; in 1954, the San-Dar Smorgasbord evolved, with the name a combination of the names of the couple's children, Sandra and Darrell. Darrell would eventually take over the business in 1981 until it closed in 1994. The smorgasbord style became unpopular or was taken over by franchises because of a change in eating habits of the general public.

The good and plentiful destination for tour buses featured one hundred different foods, over twenty hot foods and over thirty desserts. The San-Dar could seat 325 people. It was the ever-popular "all-you-can-eat" style at the time. Families would go there once a year as a special treat.

San-Dar Smorgasbord pastry shelves. *Courtesy Christine Hayes.*

The Snyder family provided many employees. Many other Bellville residents were employed there. Darrell Banks was mayor of Bellville at one time. His sister Sandra Banks Homerick is the village's tax expert. Darrell was also president of the Mayors' Association of Ohio. He personally greeted all his customers and made them feel like family. Many people are still looking for the recipes of the amazing San-Dar. Two appear—cashew nut stuffing and Dutch apple dessert—in *The Best of Lost Recipes*, by Jaya Saxena.

The "soda grill" section of the original restaurant, at this writing, is Rainbow's End Antiques. Brumby's Coffeehouse & Pizzeria is in the smorgasbord area and started in 1999. Low ceilings and covered windows were opened up to light and space by owner Bret Gandee. On Christine's site visit, it would appear Gandee has created a haven for the village's teenagers and family groups. Eclectic décor such as hanging old windowpanes, a copper samovar, an old mirror, wrought-iron leafy panels, a chess set and checkers provide atmosphere.

Gandee actually took over right from the Banks family. Darrell's wife, Marty, kept a rear portion of the building as Pizza on the Alley. This evolved into the made-from-scratch daily pizza dough and sauce and daily-roasted green coffee beans ground "On Site In Sight" of the new venue, Brumby's.

Buckeye Lake

Thirty miles east of Columbus, Buckeye Lake was built as Licking Summit Reservoir in 1826 as a feeder lake for the Ohio and Erie Canal Project. In 1835, Thomas Minthorn opened the first hotel, and by the 1910s, the renamed Buckeye Lake had an amusement park, hotels, boardinghouses, dance pavilions, ballparks and numerous water activities, serviced by the interurban railcars from Columbus.

The Lilac Room

1920s–1940s
Park Property

Like many amusement attractions of the era, Buckeye Lake was developed by a transit company, the Columbus, Buckeye Lake and Newark Traction Company, as incentive for riders on the far-reaching lines. The property was purchased from the Bounds and Swick families, and swampy areas were drained and built into lakefront facilities.

Sonny Brockway's grandfather Chauncy Brockway was manager of the Lilac Room, the largest sit-down restaurant in the park in its day. The pre-air-conditioning eating establishment was built as two stories, with the upper floor open on all four sides. Bands played Sunday afternoon concerts on this upper floor. Also, in the days before refrigeration, two deep tanks filled with ice kept the drinks cold. The elder Brockway had been a tap dancer with Al G. Field's Minstrel Show and later worked for Bott Brothers Restaurant in Columbus (later the Clock and then the Elevator Brewery at this writing), where he learned to play pool and manage restaurants. In 1918, he and his wife moved to Buckeye Lake, where he owned a poolroom in the park and managed concessions as well as the Lilac Room.

The running of things in Buckeye Lake continued into the next generation. Sonny Brockway says, "Chance Brockway [Dad] ran the Buckeye Lake Bus Station Restaurant at the park entrance, starting in 1937. He also ran the concession stand at the Mayfair Room in the Mayfair Hotel, which was destroyed by fire in the early 1950s. Grace and Bill Harrison also managed the Lilac Room, along with my grandfather."

Lilac Room restaurant. *Courtesy Sonny Brockway.*

Sonny Brockway's maternal grandfather, Howard Roley, also ran the Feedbox Restaurant in front of the Lone Star Boat Line at Buckeye Lake. There was also another Roley-owned Feedbox in Baltimore, Ohio.

Many restaurants, hotels, dance halls, concession stands and other venues came and went for decades at Buckeye Lake. Big bands gave way to teen dances held by Gene Fullen in the Crystal Ballroom in the 1960s. One dance hall, reflecting the changing times, became a theater for silent films and then a bowling alley. Along with changing tastes came the ravages of fires, floods and storms. The last days of the great amusement park and dances came in 1968. The Greater Buckeye Lake Historical Society now has a record of the exciting days of Buckeye Lake.

Chillicothe

Chillicothe was the first (1803) and third capital of Ohio. The town's name comes from the original Shawnee people. The site was the center of the ancient Hopewell culture. Later, Chillicothe was central in the Underground Railroad. Now the town hosts two annual festivals: Feast of the Flowering Moon and the Southern Ohio Storytelling Festival. Nearby are the Adena Historical Mansion and the Tecumseh! outdoor drama experience.

The Fox Farm Inn

1935–1990
1365 North Bridge Street, Route 23,
one mile north of Chillicothe

The 1843 Federal-style home built by Dr. Jonathan Miesse survived the 1913 flood, when water reached the first-floor windowsills. The house was opened in 1935 as the Fox Farm Inn by owner Carson Driesbach. It had been an actual farm for raising foxes around 1924, when mated pairs were sold to investors for $1,500. At one time, it was known as the Fox Farm Gardens. An old undated article states, "Music for dancing under the stars was provided by the Five Little Foxes. Miss May Pickens of Circleville was manager of the Gardens."

Above: Fox Farm. *Courtesy Christine Hayes.*

Left: Fox Farm ad. *Courtesy Christine Hayes.*

We know from an ad that steaks, chicken and seafood were served from 5:00 p.m. until midnight. It had an early American décor, with paintings, prints and photos of hunting dogs, horses and foxes. It was a popular place with people going to the nearby Tecumseh! pageant, as the diners were served early enough to get to the outdoor theater and see Tecumseh enter on horseback and plunge into the onstage pond.

At this writing, the old house is the site of E.M. Smith Jewelers.

Circleville

Circleville, founded in 1810, originally was laid out in a circle with the county courthouse in the center, though today the town has a standard grid pattern. The circle came from a large Hopewell culture earthwork, of which there are no remains. Circleville is famous for its pumpkin show every October and its Ted Lewis Museum. Lewis was a vaudeville performer and a bandleader.

Tink's Tavern

1946–1974
2815 North Court Street

R and N Steeles

1974–2000
2815 North Court Street

Tink's Tavern

2000–2008
2815 North Court Street

Tink's Tavern. *Courtesy Christine Hayes.*

Tink's Tavern was opened by Eldon "Tink" Hill after his service in World War II. After Tink passed away, his wife ran it for years. It specialized in fine steaks, seafood, chicken and chops. People would take a drive in the country to sample the pickerel. The eating area could accommodate 150 people, and Tink's had a party room with its own bar that could hold 70 people. The recessed bar in the main room was designed by Coburn Morgan, who also designed for the Wine Cellar and the Kahiki.

Robert and Nancy Steele took over the restaurant in 1974 and added prime rib, roast beef and spaghetti to the menu. Robert Steele had managed Tink's for ten years prior to the name change.

The establishment was later sold to Ed Webb, a local accountant, who again adopted the name Tink's. The tavern celebrated its fiftieth year under Webb's management. Webb kept the tavern alive until he passed away in 2008. At this writing, the building is still there, sitting empty.

DELAWARE

Delaware is known for Ohio Wesleyan University and the Little Brown Jug, the "anchor" horse race in the Triple Crown of Pacing (harness racing), the premier annual event of September's Delaware County Fair.

The Brown Jug Restaurant

1946–1970
21 NORTH SANDUSKY STREET

1970–2008
13 WEST WILLIAM STREET

The same year that the Little Brown Jug race had its start (1946), Spot Lowder, Noel England and Hayes Fate opened the Brown Jug as a beer bar. They lasted one year as owners of the classic Greek-fronted place, the Deposit Bank Building on North Sandusky. The year 1947 brought Gene "Buck" Lamb and his wife, Irene, as owners. When Gene passed away, his mother ran it for the next sixteen years. In 1963, it was purchased by Don "Bear" Smith and Joe Ellsworth, who owned the popular OSU campus bar the Library. Ellsworth stayed at the Library, while Smith ran the Brown Jug. Don and Peg Laaksonen purchased Ellsworth's share in 1965 and in 1968 became sole proprietors. The Laaksonens moved it around the corner to William Street in 1970. During the remodeling of the new building, they covered the display windows and the street-level front with redwood siding. The community elders, known as the "Rusty Zipper Bunch," met here for lunch.

Bill Stroud and Edward Wolf purchased the building and business on September 12, 1970. In 1989, they removed the redwood front and restored the original Italianate architectural style. This heralded the change from college bar to family restaurant. In 2004, they added patio seating and in 2005 introduced the tenting and lighting of that area.

Stroud and Wolf were proud to receive the 2000 Midwest Foodservice News award for being judged one of the five best restaurants in Ohio. They had also been named Small Business of the Year by the Delaware Chamber of Commerce in 1998 and later received the Ohio Main Street Business of the Year in 2006 by the State Agency for Downtown Ohio.

Don "Bear" Smith, the part owner of the Brown Jug starting in the early 1960s (when it was at 21 North Sandusky), sold his interest and went on to the Campbell House on South Sandusky in Delaware. Smith had at one time been drafted by and trained with a pro football team (but never played) and was most proud of playing on the national championship team of Miami of Ohio. Smith and eight people also opened a restaurant and bar at Miami called the Purity. Smith returned to the Brown Jug as a cook, after three years' absence, when it moved to William Street.

Smith had memorized all the recipes. When he had heart bypass surgery in the early 1990s, Wolf visited him in the hospital and pumped him for the recipes. "For the first time, we put the recipes down in black-and-white. Bear had the gift of spice," says Wolf. Wolf's niece has since begun to duplicate the recipes for smaller quantities.

Ohio Wesleyan University named Stroud and Wolf honorary alumni. The two backed several school levies and had spaghetti dinners for levy campaigns. Delaware's mayor proclaimed April 21, 2006, the restaurant's sixtieth anniversary, Brown Jug Restaurant Day.

Unfortunately, the Brown Jug did not last but two years more. Hoggy's, which had taken over the catering at the Little Brown Jug race, took over the space after 2008. After that, in 2012, a new venue called Brooklyn Heights Bar & Grill opened in the site. The bar and oak dining booths were restored to their original condition. Brooklyn Heights also obtained two original Brown Jug tables. At this writing, the William Street site is sitting empty. The original pillared place on Sandusky is home to the Delaware County Board of Realtors at this writing.

Greg Cielec, a former Brown Jug employee and Ohio Wesleyan graduate, gathered recipes, memories and photos for a cookbook of the extensive menu, including pizza, sandwiches, subs, soups, spaghetti, steaks and seafood. Among the well-loved soups were Jamaican red bean, poorman's and cheeseburger. Among the favorite desserts was the bread pudding. At one time, the Brown Jug had sixty-five employees, including part-timers. At least one or two were always Ohio Wesleyan students.

Granville

Granville was founded in 1805. Early institutions and seminaries evolved into what is now Denison University. The village is noted for its historic New England architecture.

Bryn Mawr

1973–1995
3758 Lancaster Road

Elias Fassett, president of the Central Ohio Railroad in 1849, built a large Italianate mansion south of Granville. "Fassett's Folly" included solid brick walls, twelve-foot ceilings, marble fireplaces, crystal chandeliers, a third-floor ballroom and a cupola on the roof. It is said Fassett walked his widow's walk on the roof so he could wave a lantern at the evening train; the engineer was supposed to respond by blowing the whistle. After Fassett died in 1854, the house went through several owners, acquiring the name Bryn Mawr about 1890 and a Colonial Revival portico and balcony sometime after 1911. It went through periods of being a girls' school, a school for the mentally retarded and a nursing home before it became a renovated restaurant in 1973.

Bryn Mawr means "big hill" in Welsh. There was a great barn next to the house that had the name spelled out in slate tiles. Gale Douglass, who worked at Bryn Mawr from 1973 to 1977, remembers the barn burning down. She also remembers the costume she and the other servers wore: an 1800s-style long dress, period wallpaper-print in pale yellow with small pink flowers. She especially remembers the windows, with original shutters folding into the sides.

Bryn Mawr was a destination for American and continental cuisine and country ambience. A huge awning covered the terrace amid spectacular plantings. Inside, the cream and green motif and more plantings and flowers were reflected in the mirrors and chandeliers. The former summer kitchen and laundry in the basement became the less formal "Dave's Dig," where nightly entertainment was provided by Mike Williams at his Bosendorfer piano, a remarkable German instrument. The basement floor had to be excavated eighteen inches so it could be a viable venue.

Favorite menu items included homemade cinnamon rolls, three onion soup, veal, lamb, seafood, chicken potpie, the creamy onion salad

Bryn Mawr. *Courtesy Marty Godbey.*

dressing and sautéed Norwegian salmon served with a minted cucumber Hollandaise. Owners David and Dottie Klauder also provided shops on the lane, where crafts, antiques, plants and herbs were sold to make a country outing complete. Manager and greeter Philomena Dolan and manager Jim Hendrix made the customer feel comfortable.

The venue is at this writing a rentable party house.

Jacksontown

Jacksontown is an unincorporated community in Licking County. It is the birthplace of Carl Osburn, who held the record for the most career Olympic medals by an American man from 1920 to 2008. Osburn competed in shooting in 1912, 1920 and 1924, winning five gold medals and several silver and bronze.

Clark's Dining Room

1918–2009

6811 National Road, Jacksontown

Clark's Dining Room started out as Clark's Hotel. The thirteen-room operation was built in the early 1800s on the site of a former stagecoach stop at the corner of the National Road and State Route 13. Besides the thirteen rooms, the hotel had a pool room, a bar, a lunch counter and a barbershop.

In 1918, Harry and Clara Clark packed their bags from nearby Lakeside, where they operated a boardinghouse that catered to visitors to Buckeye Lake, and purchased the hotel. They also lived in the hotel until 1929. Their grandson Tom Clark related that the place was pretty lively and a popular place for local farmers to congregate, along with hustlers on their way along the National Road.

Tom's father, Ray Clark, was a little boy when the family lived there and a pretty good pool player. When hobos and pool hustlers would come in and begin to clean out the locals in pool bets, Ray was offered up as the next player. Tom tells the story that the pool shark would allow Ray to win at first but would begin to up the stakes as the night went on. Ray was a pool prodigy and easily kept up with the men making the bets. As the sun started to go down and Ray was winning, one of the bartenders would

Clark's Restaurant. *Courtesy Tom Clark.*

holler at Ray something to the effect of "Ray! Don't you have school tomorrow? Get yourself to bed!" When he heard this, Ray would dash up to bed—winnings in hand. The hustler would then be left without any ill-gotten gain and would eventually leave and go on down the road. At that point, young Ray would come down and give the farmers back all the money they had lost.

Additionally, the barbershop was more than it appeared. Apparently, before the state-run lottery, lots of places ran "numbers" games, and the Clark's Hotel barbershop was the Jacksontown numbers drop.

In 1933, Harry Clark passed away, leaving Clara to run the place with the assistance of many dedicated employees. This was also during the Depression, and "Grandma" Clark, as she came to be called, was always a Good Samaritan, offering work to the many folks who came by looking for a job in return for a meal. It wasn't uncommon for the sidewalk to be swept four times in a day or the leaves to be raked half a dozen. People who knew her would question Grandma about this, and her reply was, "If you take away a man's pride, you take away his self-respect. If he earns his meal, he'll keep his pride and his self-respect."

Similarly, in 1924, a young lady by the name of Florence was waiting for a bus at a bus stop across from the hotel. Grandma Clark saw that she was upset and asked her what was the matter. Florence explained that she was bound for OSU as a co-ed, and she didn't want to go, but her parents insisted she attend. Seeing how upset she was, Clara offered her a job if she wanted it. She accepted and came to live and work with the Clarks (and took on the name of "Aunt Flo") at the hotel first and then the Dining Room. She stayed until she passed away in 1984 at the age of seventy-nine!

Things at the hotel were going along fine until Labor Day 1954, when tragedy struck: a fire burned the hotel to the ground. Apparently, this awful day didn't even faze Grandma Clark, who reportedly said at the time, "As soon as the darned thing stops burning, I want to build a Dining Room." At the age of seventy-eight, that's exactly what she proceeded to do. She continued to own and operate Clark's Dining Room and built a small bungalow home next door with a sidewalk in the back that connected to the restaurant.

It was at that point that her son Ray and his sister Thelma took over the reins. They became known for their fried chicken and homemade pies. They offered three main menu items at the time: fried chicken, ham and steak, along with sides of homemade mashed potatoes, vegetables and rolls. But it was the butterscotch pies, cherry pies, coconut cream pics and so many more that kept folks coming back to Clark's Dining Room—often waiting in line for more than an hour.

And the place didn't even have a cash register. Tom shared that Clark's only had a cashbox, and they kept track of the orders on a legal pad in the back. When folks would come up to pay for their meal, they simply told them which of the three entrées they had, and his dad or aunt would determine how much they ate and charge accordingly.

Also of note, when the cooks and staff got tired and wanted to go home, they would start to tell folks they had run out of chicken—even though they had plenty—in order to close down the place for the night!

In 1987, after a two-year stint in the army and a career as the manager of the Cleveland Convention Center, the Ohio State Fair and the Arizona State Fair, Ray asked Tom if he would take over the restaurant, which he did. For the first two years, he put nearly all of the profits back into the place to modernize it. He added new linoleum, new ovens, new dishes (purchased secondhand for $150 in nearby Roseville) and even a cash register.

The reputation of Clark's delicious home-cooked food began to spread, and the place had regulars who would show up every Sunday for a decade to get their day started. Tom recalls, "One couple came the first Sunday of every month from Pittsburgh!" The servers and cooks knew what to expect and had their tables, drinks and appetizers ready for them.

All kinds of folks would show up. Vince Gill was a regular when he would visit his dad. Hal Block of Block's Bagels would often call up and say, "Chicken [Tom], I've got seven tonight. Seven o'clock okay?" That party was often made up of the Block family and the Tsao family of Kahiki fame. Even Les Wexner's mother, Bella Wexner, was a regular, and Tom was always glad of her visits. When other guests would get excited and ask Tom if he knew who that was, he would quietly tell them, "Yes, she's a wonderful lady. The only difference between you and her is that you tip better!" and he and the customer would have a gentle laugh.

But as costs began to increase and new regulations were put in place, the family made the difficult decision to close Clark's Dining Room in 2008. Author Doug Motz and his family were some of those folks who made the trek from Reynoldsburg to Clark's on a very regular basis, and they definitely had to have one more meal of fried chicken and homemade cherry pie before the place closed.

When Tom Clark did sell Clark's Dining Room, the only stipulations he made to the new owners were that it couldn't be a restaurant and it couldn't be called Clark's. That was a bit of a tough pill to swallow for the new owner—also named Tom Clark (no relation), who as of this writing runs a successful sports bar on the site of the legendary Clark's Dining Room.

Marion

Marion was a railroad hub and a stop for travelers on Route 23 from Toledo to Columbus. It is noted for the Marion Steam Shovel Company (later Marion Power Shovel) and the Spanish Colonial Revival–style Palace Theatre, built in 1928 and in continuous use. The twenty-ninth president, Warren G. Harding, built a home in Marion in 1890 and ran his newspaper, and then his campaign, from the front porch. Harding's home and the Harding Memorial can be visited in Marion.

Café George (also named the Crest Coffee Shop and the Keg and Vine)

1946–2008
131 South Main Street

"Café George serves both sides of the aisle," says George Kasotis of a sign that used to hang in his restaurant. Several governors and senators frequently stopped in, among other politicians, as well as John Glenn when he was traveling by car, not spaceship.

The site of the former Café George was also the site of Amos Kling's dry goods store, built in 1832. His daughter, Florence Kling, became the wife of President Warren G. Harding. The building was torn down in the 1910s and replaced with a newer business block, but the site of her birth (she was born upstairs, where the Klings lived above their store) is a place where people have gathered at the versatile Kasotis restaurant for decades, as is the site of her grave, the Harding Memorial, a few blocks away.

George Kasotis was born in the kitchen. His parents owned the Pleasant Inn in the nearby town of Caledonia. His mother was the cook, and his father was a cobbler. She would serve sandwiches and Old Dutch beer while George's father repaired the shoes of the client. When it was time for George to be born, the doctor came in his horse and buggy, guzzled brandy and assisted in the birth on a blanket in the restaurant kitchen.

In 1942, the grown-up George and his mother started a restaurant together in the Dulcinger Building at 176 South Main Street in Marion and called it the Home Café. When the former Hamburg King (popular in the 1930s and '40s) site came up for sale at 131 South Main Street, they started the Crest Coffee Shop there in 1946. For three or four years, they ran the two places and then finally gave up the Home Café.

George came back from serving in the Korean War (he was drafted and then wounded but came back healthy after two years) and headed straight for Lazarus, then located in downtown Columbus only, for some Italian clothes and a Borsolino hat to top them off. He wanted to look sharp as a civilian. He asked some employees of Lazarus where they ate; they replied, "Doersam's." So George headed there for lunch and got a job. He remembers it fondly but also remembers that they called his boss, Clyde Doersam, "the Bull."

George's mother did not want alcohol in the Crest, saying, "The church people won't come." Finally in the 1960s, when there was an oil boom in the town of Marion, George transformed the Crest into the Keg and Vine. George recalls, "In 150 feet of space, I had 75 feet of bar with beer and 75 feet of dining room serving wine with dinner."

The restaurant at 131 South Main occupied George and his wife, Joan—who is of Swiss descent, from Fairborn, Ohio—for many years. It was Joan's idea to rename it the Café George in 1983, the year they married. The kitchen was moved out of the center of the restaurant to the front, where it was open and inviting.

At this writing, the venue is the Baires Restaurante. Of it, George comments, "I taught Marcella of Buenos Aires [the present proprietor] all my Greek tricks."

Mount Gilead

U.S. Route 42 was one of the main traffic arteries between Cleveland and Cincinnati, running right through Mount Gilead. Fine dining, as later recommended by food critic Duncan Hines, could be enjoyed on Mount Gilead's main square at the Globe Hotel or the Inn. Also, the Leaf held forth on Route 95 for decades.

The Leaf Restaurant

1962-2006
6022 State Route 95

The Warren Gordon family opened a Sohio gas station next to the future site of the Leaf in 1960. Mark Gordon, one of the three sons of Warren Gordon, remembers pumping gas, checking oil and washing car windshields for passing motorists, as was the "full-service" style of the day. The station was busy, and the route had very few restaurants (Daugherty's of Mansfield was one) along the well-traveled Cleveland–Cincinnati corridor.

In January 1962, the Gordons opened a modern restaurant for the times in classy turquoise and orange décor similar to Howard Johnson's. Ken Carlson was the architect for the Leaf. It cost $75,000 to build. Mark remembers opening day as a "snow day" from school, so his great-aunt picked him up and brought him to the new restaurant, where he washed dishes. He was fifteen.

Mark continued as a cashier; he would also "meet, greet, seat and water down" the customers. Even when he went off to college, he worked summers and holidays at the Leaf, as did his brother, Stephen. Mark eventually married, and both he and his wife began teaching in Delaware. In March 1973, he and his wife moved back to Mount Gilead to a house they had

The Leaf. *Courtesy Christine Hayes.*

always wanted to own. Two months later, his mother passed away, and Mark and his wife resigned their teaching positions and took over the restaurant.

The Leaf featured a maple-sugaring mural painted by Mrs. Glen Moss. The Gordons had been a farm family and had tapped trees for syrup. The good homemade food was a draw for travelers; they loved the homemade pies and rolls. And, of course, good maple syrup for pancakes!

Kenley Players celebrities would stop by on their way between Warren and Columbus. Ozzie and David Nelson from *Ozzie and Harriet*, a *Brady Bunch* actor and Geraldo Rivera are ones that Mark remembers.

By 1997, Mark had decided to quit the restaurant business and leased it out; there was a time he took it back in 2003–4 and then sold it in 2005, and the enterprise was done in 2006. The mom-and-pop restaurant business was dying due to the proliferation of fast-food plazas along the highway. The pace of life was bypassing the once trendy Leaf. A Subway now occupies the site.

The Globe Hotel Dining Room

1869–1966
Corner of North Main and North Streets,
on the Mount Gilead Square

J.F. Stone founded the Globe Hotel. It went through multiple owners and was remodeled many times. Among the hotel's notable guests were Presidents McKinley, Grant and Harding and John Philip Sousa. In the hotel's last days, an oil boom in Morrow County filled its rooms with workers. Sadly, a series of fires led to its demise, culminating in a large kitchen fire. The building was razed, and the site became a Marathon gas station. At this writing, the site is also occupied by an H&R Block business.

The Inn

1930s–1960s
16 North Main Street

1960s–1989
Kimmey property, two miles northeast on Route 42

The Inn, standing for close to thirty years on the northeast corner of Mount Gilead's central square, was originally called Lotilla's. About 1942, the restaurant was taken over by Lloyd and Dorothy Kimmey. Lloyd was a Morrow County native, and Dorothy was a native of Essex, Ontario. Dorothy was an amazing cook; soon, there were lines outside the door of her inn.

People drove there for special occasions. Families came every Sunday and had their reserved table. Some of the "made from scratch" specialties were lemon meringue pie, turkey roll, peach jam and scalloped cabbage. Thanksgiving dinner was served, and then after that, the Inn closed until Easter Sunday.

After eighteen years, the Inn became the site of a bank, so the Kimmeys moved the restaurant to their home property. They enlarged their enterprise; they had several rooms, among them the Fireplace Room, the Patio Room and the Pergola. Here, Dorothy could make apple butter on site in her copper kettles. The Kimmeys could have a "Chuck Wagon

Santa at the Inn. *Courtesy the Morrow County Historical Society.*

Bob Hope and Dorothy and Lloyd Kimmey at the Inn, September 15, 1952. *Courtesy Al Tozer.*

Buffet." The surroundings were beautiful yet homey, with antique plates and glassware in well-lighted shelves. Ivy grew on the ceiling.

Some of the Inn's famous guests were Governor Lausche, Senator Robert Taft and J.C. Penney himself. But the Inn's most famous and frequent guest was Bob Hope. Hope's brothers Fred and Sydney developed the nearby Pines Restaurant and Motel in 1946 and operated these until 1962, when traffic was redirected onto Interstate 71. So Bob Hope had a great love for Mount Gilead and the Inn. Hope had a special signed red-and-black chair at the Inn, and a dollar bill signed by Hope was always on display.

The Inn finally closed in 1989, due to Dorothy's declining health and advanced age. At this writing, the site of the Inn is a field where balloon rides are based.

Newark

Newark is known for its prehistoric Earthworks, now a National Historic Landmark, built by the Hopewells from 100 BC to AD 500. It has been determined that these Earthworks were used for astronomical observations and that there was also a Great Hopewell Road to the area of what is now Chillicothe. Newark was settled in 1802 by General William C. Schenck. The Ohio and Erie Canal project was begun nearby in the 1820s. The Heisey Glass Company was established here in 1895 and closed in 1957, and now there is a museum of its products in Newark.

The Sparta Restaurant

1900–2016, closed for a time
15 North Third Street, corner of Locust and
North Second Street, 16 West Main Street

The Sparta first opened as an ice cream parlor and candy store in 1900. The first owner was Christopher Baruxes. The venue was named for the hometown of his wife (he was from Corinth). Sparta was managed from 1932 to 1962 by their son, Peter C. Baruxes. Later, the management went to Peter's son, Chris James Baruxes.

The Sparta Restaurant and Brux Candy Company (jointly operated) moved several times. The one most people remember, 16 West Main Street, opened in 1949. The ownership changed hands in 1988, from the Baruxes family to Daisy Estep, who had worked at the restaurant as both a server and a hostess for ten years. The iconic Statue of Liberty out front and the eclectic interior décor were to continue for a while.

The Sparta closed for a time and then was reopened in 2012 by Chris Ramsey as a coffee shop/restaurant. Project Main Street, with Allen Schwartz as acting president, asked for community support for a new goal for Sparta, as a "transitional workplace," a place where people who had been previously incarcerated, mostly women, could gain work skills with on-the-job training. At that time, Sparta was truly a community meeting place and had specials like meatloaf and eggs and chicken and waffles.

However, when construction began in 2016 on the Downtown Newark Square, the Sparta was too hard to get to and was forced to close its doors for lack of business. The antique candy boxes were given out as souvenirs to loyal customers. At this writing, the building has been purchased and is rumored to be getting a facelift for a new restaurant to open.

New Lexington

New Lexington is the county seat of Perry County. Januarious MacGahan, journalist and national hero of Bulgaria, is from New Lexington.

Shirley's (formerly Dunkle's)

1970s
100 West Broadway Street

Shirley's became "Pinky's" in the filming of *Brubaker* in 1979. It was owned by Lee and Shirley Ratliff. *Brubaker*, released in 1980, is an American prison drama directed by Stuart Rosenberg. Newly arrived Warden Henry Brubaker, played by Robert Redford, attempts to clean up a corrupt penal system. The screenplay was written by W.D. Richter from the 1969 book *Accomplices to the Crime: The Arkansas Prison Scandal* by Tom Murton and Joe Hyams. The film was nominated for Best Original Screenplay at the 1981 Academy Awards. The film begins with Redford posing as a prisoner (before he discloses he is the warden) and fighting with deranged prisoner Morgan Freeman.

Other Ohio filming locations were R&D Hilltop Lumber (then Howdeyshell Lumber) in New Lexington, Junction City Prison in Junction City and the Fairfield County Fairgrounds in Lancaster. The opening scene of a prison bus departure depicts the Columbus skyline and a view up South Front Street.

Following the film's facelift of Shirley's, the venue became the Chuckwagon, then was empty for a time and then was reopened as the Pizza Place by owner Vic Paini in 1983. The jukebox was replaced by televisions and satellite radio. The huge pink pig is on the wall. Throughout the Pizza Place are pictures and articles from the film production, a marquee in the front foyer and the hot-pink Pinky's neon sign in the back dining room. Former windows have been turned into shadow boxes to display art from Perry County high schoolers. The floor is original restored wood from Dunkle's, where customers danced to live music in the back room.

SPRINGFIELD

Springfield was established in 1801 by Kentuckian James Demint at the junction of the Mad River and Buck Creek. The wife of Ohio's symbolic frontiersman, Simon Kenton, named the city in honor of the many springs in the area. It is the home of Wittenberg University.

Jim's Fountain Service

1923–1978
117 SOUTH LIMESTONE STREET

Jim Georges was famous for his grilled ham sandwiches. He came to Springfield, and his fame, by a circuitous route.

He was brought to America in 1912 as a fifteen-year-old, from his native Canea on the Greek island of Crete. His father processed olive oil from his farm and had a vineyard. Jim traveled with an uncle to New Jersey, Chicago and then Terre Haute to work in a friend's confectionery. The friend moved to Springfield to work in the Sugar Bowl Restaurant downtown. The friend wrote to Jim and said there was an opening in the Olympia, a soda fountain/confectionery at 7 West Main Street. By 1916, Jim was working at the Crystal Restaurant on Limestone, in the Bookwalter Building.

By 1923, Jim had opened his own fountain. There were all grades of sundae: fancy, nut and not-so-fancy. But the attraction was the sandwiches and Jim's secret recipes for chopped olive and nut spread and ham, tuna, chicken and egg salad spreads. Sue Stuckey remembers, "Jim's sat next to the Regent Theatre. I always had an egg salad sandwich and a chocolate milkshake. But lots of kids loved the grilled cheese or the grilled ham. We kids from Springfield High School filled the booths and the stools on our way home. Jim was always cranky. If you were too loud, he threw you out."

Jim was known for his "firm word." There was no jukebox, but Karen Klingbeil LaValley remembers being entertained by epic fights between Jim and his girlfriend. There was a year in the late 1950s when Jim sold out and moved to a shop in Piqua. But he came back and took over his restaurant again.

Jim couldn't eat ham, but he bought tons of it when the business was most brisk during World War II. He recalled that as many as "five hundred cases of canned ham a year, six twelve-pound hams to a case," would come through the restaurant. He also used up 250 gallons of olives per year. He made limeade, lemonade and orange juice from fresh fruit daily. Jim worked twelve to fourteen hours six days a week—the fate of a small one-man show.

At this writing, Jim's and the Regent Theatre are sitting empty.

Westerville

Westerville is known for Otterbein University (established 1839); the homes that were part of the Underground Railroad; the Hanby House, a state memorial to composer Benjamin Hanby; and its role in the temperance movement. Westerville was the headquarters for the Anti-Saloon League. The league is now a museum attached to the library, and it is only recently that the town has allowed liquor in its establishments. Here are two iconic Westerville restaurants.

The Williams Grill

1887–1927
12–16 West College Avenue

1927-1975
14 North State Street

Williams Bakery and Confectionery began in 1887 and stayed in the family for four generations: J.R. Williams (founder), C.F. "Pete" Williams, J.R. "Bud" Williams and J.R. "John" Williams.

Originally a horse-and-wagon delivery bakery business, the first J.R. era led to the Williams Ice Cream Company, an 1890s soda fountain and ice cream parlor, popular with Otterbein students. The focus on the bakery ended in 1913. A sandwich menu was added, and in 1927, in conjunction with the move to State Street, a full three-meals-a-day restaurant emerged, with a modern ice cream plant in the rear. An electric sign blazed: "Ice Cream Soda with the Foam Floating Out." The banquet hall, on the second floor, could hold large groups. It was called the Crystal Room, so named because of its chandeliers and wall lamps. The establishment, though still hosting students, became less of a hangout and more of a fine dining experience for families and businesspeople.

The restaurant was packed on Ohio State game days and during the Ohio State Fair, as it was located on the famous "3C" Highway, a major thoroughfare to and from Columbus. People are still talking about the lemon meringue pie. In the early 1940s, the dining room was redone in a more "modern" look, and the basement became "The Pit," a place for teenagers with a jukebox and a dance floor. In 1955 came more remodeling, now known as the "classic '50's" look, with new booths and formica instead of marble countertops.

In 1969, owners outside the family, Pat and Ernie Ernsberger, restored the restaurant to its elegant former appearance. Pat had worked at the Grill several times. The Ernsbergers kept all the long-employed staff. They sold in 1971 to contractor Bill Klusty.

Klusty upped the technology of the entire building and accomplished a remodel into a "Gay Nineties" motif, with quick-order foods, pizza and silent movies. The restaurant was renamed William's Original Soda Parlour Restaurant. The Crystal Room became a smorgasbord.

In 1973, Klusty sold to Dave Hoodin, who closed it in 1975. Klusty bought it back, with two architects, and converted it into the Alley Shoppes. The utmost Westerville gathering place was gone.

Some more facts: in the early 1940s, Pete Williams was the president of the Ohio Restaurant Association. At one time, the Greyhound Bus Company business was taken care of at the Williams cash register. There was always a candy and a cigar counter, and salted nuts were roasted in the kitchen at all times. A grand piano stood in the upstairs lounge. The restaurant adjoined the State Street Theatre. At this writing, the State Street Theatre is the 8 State Bistro, a restaurant with movie-themed décor and silent films projected on the wall; the hostess is stationed as if at a box office.

The stained-glass windows from the last incarnation of the Williams Grill/ William's decorated Pasquale's Pizza, one of the Alley Shoppes. Pasquale's ended in 2015. At this writing, at the old site of Williams Grill is the Asterisk Supper Club, with a library of seven thousand books, a bar brought from Nevada and historical menus and photos of the Williams eras on the walls.

Buzz Cockrell's

Late 1960s–1995
1 North State Street

James M. "Buzz" Cockrell worked the front of his classic hometown restaurant while his wife, Mary Jean Carfagna Cockrell, presided over the kitchen. Buzz was a realtor in his other profession. At one time, Buzz was the mayor of Minerva Park (a nearby municipality); he served two terms as the president of the Central Ohio Restaurant Association and was the president of the Ohio Restaurant Association.

"CORA [Central Ohio Restaurant Association] Elects." Buzz Cockrell at left, Tom Kanatas center. *Courtesy Kanatas family.*

Buzz had also owned the Jimchuck Restaurant at 1948 Cleveland Avenue in Westerville. At this writing, the site is the Trojan Motorcycle Club. Unfortunately, we have no dates for this venue. Cockrell was also involved in Six Pence School, which served children with learning disabilities. Many of these students worked at his restaurant for fifteen to twenty years. Cockrell was active in numerous activities of the Westerville community, including St. Paul the Apostle Church, Knights of Columbus and the O Club at Otterbein.

Buzz Cockrell's was known for its homemade salad dressings and lasagna noodles. The restaurant was also known for its Ole Buzzard Club, a group of local businessmen who met there on a regular basis. In 1985, Buzz Cockrell's was sold to Ken Baumgarter, who sold it to Tony Aponte, its last owner in 1994. Aponte changed the name to the Village Cupboard, which just wasn't the same. That lasted for just a year. At this writing, it is a location of the popular Graeter's Ice Cream.

Worthington

Worthington was founded in 1803 by settlers who came from Granby, Connecticut, in wagons, led by James Kilbourne. The town is named after Thomas Worthington, who later became governor of Ohio. Worthington's Village Green and several beautifully restored buildings survive from the early founding. The town is completely surrounded by Columbus. Linworth is included in the town limits (see the Elmwood Restaurant and Victoria Station). Worthington is known for its extensive year-round, weekly farmers' market.

The Hearth & Eagle

1975–1999

7800 Olentangy River Road, Olentangy Valley Shopping Center

The Hearth & Eagle was the centerpiece of Don Herb's restaurant career. He was also the proprietor of the Clock (1954–71; it went on to new ownership) and the manager of the OSU Faculty Club (1972–75, in the height of the Woody Hayes era). Herb was a member of the Food Services Executives Association and received these awards: Restaurateur of the Year from the Central Ohio Restaurant Association and a Lifetime Achievement Award from the Ohio Restaurant Association.

The Hearth & Eagle was designed and owned originally by Clem Ambrose of Dublin and Tom Mahle of Worthington. The name and atmosphere was based on a book by Anya Seton, published in 1948, *The Hearth and Eagle*, about the Honeywood family who arrived in Salem, Massachusetts, in 1626 and built the original tavern in Marblehead, Massachusetts, in 1629. Stout food and drink, warmth and good cheer made the tavern a haven for the sailors of the Grand Banks fishing fleet. The actual home is still in the hands of the descendants (says an article from 1974), the Browns, but it is no longer a tavern.

Hearth & Eagle matchbook. *Courtesy Christine Hayes.*

After a few years, Herb purchased the business from Ambrose and Mahle. According to his daughter, Donna Herb, the only day he missed being in the H&E was the day his beloved dog died, and the only day the place was closed was the day his brother, Carl, died. Herb's wife, Louise, or "Mama Lou," as she was known, was a great cook. Some of her specialties were soups, salads, biscuit strawberry shortcake, Dutch apple pie with pecan topping, lemon meringue pie, rhubarb pie and strawberry pie. Regulars always knew to ask for "Lou's Special of the Day" before looking at the regular menu. Donna reports that at her mother's funeral, Lou's coveted recipes were handed out.

Donna credits her mother for having a flair for creating amazing flower arrangements and centerpieces for parties. Lou could make a baby buggy out of a watermelon for baby showers and a Christmas tree of shrimp. Donna says, "One of the Herbs always had to be at the front door to greet." Everyone received a relish tray of fresh vegetables when they were seated. Donna's brother Steve worked there, as did their cousin Jeff, Carl's son. A favorite starter or whole meal could be made of the ham and bean soup created by Chef Michael Farner.

Like the original, the Worthington Hearth & Eagle offered the warmth of food, drink and a live fire in a huge hearth from 11:00 a.m. to 1:30 a.m. Some décor details included candles, red cloths, wooden beams and, above the fireplace, a replica of the United States Constitution, executed by hand by a friend of the owner. At the entrance was an eagle from Marblehead, Massachusetts. A long bar was reflected in a mirror, which, in turn, surrounded a picture of the famous sloop the *Cutty Sark*. This same bar was the first in Ohio to feature Heineken on draft, a big deal for its day.

Appropriate paintings decorated the dining room and the party room. Entertainment was provided at times by Kelly Crum Delaveris and a brother-sister act called Clyde & Hilda. The banquet room had originally been an art gallery next door. The Herbs knocked out the wall when the art gallery went out of business. Donna laughingly refers to herself and her sibling and cousin as the dumbwaiters who ran up and down the stairs to serve those in the private party room.

Especially well remembered is the Christmas décor at the Hearth & Eagle. Channel 4 would come to film there at holiday time. Don Herb would always purchase a theme-decorated tree from the Festival of Trees, which benefited the Columbus Children's Hospital. The banquet room and everywhere would be loaded with Lou's flair for decoration, and the Herbs booked many private holiday parties. Donna has a story about the time *PM Magazine* came to film: the fireplace was so big that it had the biggest flue in the city. Santa had to wait in the chimney for an interminable time, as there were constant breaks for segments and commercials. Finally, Santa came down, and local singer Hilda Doyle sang appropriate songs and children flocked. One assumes the fire was not kindled at the time!

Donna's other stories center on the OSU game days, when brunch would be served at the H&E and then all boarded a bus to the game and were brought back for dinner. "Dad had connections for good tickets through his former job at the Faculty Club." Donna was in charge of finding everyone after the game and directing them to the bus—quite a feat. Donna reports that when Woody's successor, Earle Bruce, had a winning game, he ate at the Jai Lai. When the OSU team lost, Bruce ate at the H&E. (Bruce was a resident of nearby Worthington Hills.) Steve Herb was in charge of keeping people who wanted to tell Bruce what he did wrong away from the coach while he was trying to eat.

When the Worthington Hills neighborhood had its huge Independence Day celebration and fireworks, it was a big day and night at the H&E. Outdoor seating and, indeed, the whole parking lot was filled with revelers. The Hearth & Eagle also was known for swinging St. Patrick's Day celebrations.

Toward the end of the 1990s, Herb sold the restaurant to Tom and Marty Brown, and Hank and Carol Helling. Tom Brown had been an executive at Lazarus and was the brother of Ohio attorney general Bill Brown. Tim Miller was a friend of the son, Terry Brown, and Tim had a job in the summer of 1999 as a dishwasher, busboy and server. He remembers the prime rib and ribs and Hank Helling singing an a capella version of "Mack the Knife" every night.

Donna moved to working a few doors down at the Hills Market, where she works to this day. She still does catering and bartending. It was a sad day when she had to witness the bulldozers entering the front of the former H&E to remodel it as the Rusty Bucket. The site at this writing is still the Rusty Bucket.

Chapter 8

L'ARMAGNAC AND L'ANTIBES

L'Armagnac

1976–1987
121 South Sixth Street, Columbus

L'Antibes

1993–2015
772 North High Street, Suite 106, Columbus

Sometimes, despite our very best efforts, a story or fact we gather isn't quite what we thought it was, and so is the case for our history of L'Armagnac from our first book, *Lost Restaurants of Columbus, Ohio*. As a follow-up, our friend Dale was very gracious and gave us a terrific interview. What follows is the story from Dale, with our sincere appreciation to him for allowing us to set the record straight!

L'Armagnac was opened in 1976 in the space that had once housed a Hungarian lunch spot known as Ilonka's Encore. Dale Gussett and Douglas Johnson bought it from Ilonka's owner Helen McClain.

Gussett and Johnson had met at the Culinary Institute of America, where both of them graduated in 1973. Dale received a fellowship and taught for an additional year, and Doug worked at the five-star Harold's restaurant in upstate New York. After a year of that, the pair moved to New York, where Dale was an assistant manager and Doug was a purchasing manager at the venerable Waldorf Astoria.

After a stint there, the pair moved to Providence, Rhode Island, where Dale worked as the chef at a small French restaurant called Pot au Feu. While there, Dale's father contacted them about Ilonka's being for sale, and they moved to Columbus to open up their own business.

While students, they had operated a small catering business. And as there were no authentic French restaurants in Columbus at the time—the closest were Pigall's and the Maisonette in Cincinnati—the idea seemed quite sound. The concept was similar to that of Pot au Feu: a pre-fixe menu of $7.50 or $9.50, depending on your entrée choice. There were always at least six appetizers, two or three soups, nine or ten entrées and at least six desserts to choose from; a choice from each category was included in the price.

Dale shared:

> *Our first day in business we opened at 5:00 p.m. and did not get any customers until 7:30. They walked in and saw the restaurant was empty and asked me if I would like them to leave. Of course, I asked them to please stay. They did, and they enjoyed the meal very much. It turned out to be Robert and Hattie Lazarus!*
>
> *Word got around, and business continued to grow. Eventually, we were reviewed by* Columbus Monthly, *the* Columbus Citizen-Journal *and the* Dispatch. *Reservations were required most nights and on weekends usually a few weeks in advance. Eventually, the* Chicago Tribune *and the* New York Times *wrote about the restaurant, as well as all of the Ohio newspapers.*

Customers included Robert Redford, Anne Miller, Paul Lynde, Mitzi Gaynor and several others who appeared at Kenley Players. L'Armagnac also catered to Grant Hospital doctors and employees, university professors and business executives. "We were proud to employ a large number of people from the gay community that were discriminated against by many employers at the time," said Dale.

Dale and Doug were co-owners as well as co-chefs, and one was always on site during the hours the restaurant was open. Signature dishes included ris de veau à la creme, tournedoes forestiere, cervelle de veau grenobloise, faison demidoff and rouget en papillote with sauce mousseline.

Dale and Doug decided to sell in 1982, as they could not come to agreement about how they wanted the restaurant to proceed. John Bessey and Tom Johnson bought it and continued to run it for another five years. Dale and Doug sold the building in 1987. Today, the site is occupied by the William Wilkins Professional Building across from Grant Hospital.

L'Antibes was located at 772 North High Street, Suite 106. It was opened in February 1993 by co-owners Dale Gussett and Larry Williamson. Dale directed the back of the house and Larry the front and all accounting duties. The atmosphere was often described as romantic and intimate. Many people considered it a "special occasion" restaurant, and there were numerous engagements and other celebrations there.

Some of the popular dishes were shrimp Orleanaise; tournedoes with shallots, brandy and Roquefort demi-glace; and lobster with leeks and saffron beurre blanc.

Larry and Dale sold it in July 2007 to Matt Litzinger. He continued to operate as L'Antibes until May 2015, when he decided to change the concept; it is now known as Homefare.

Chapter 9

KAHIKI

A FINAL CHAPTER?

1961–2000
3583 East Broad Street, Columbus

This is the restaurant that started it all. Doug was asked to write up a Polynesian restaurant in Columbus called the Grass Skirt back in 2012 as part of his "History Lesson" series for columbusunderground.com. That column eventually led to his writing a book, *Kahiki Supper Club: A Polynesian Paradise in Columbus, Ohio*, with David Meyers, Elise Meyers-Walker and Jeff Chenault—which, in turn, led to our writing *Lost Restaurants of Columbus, Ohio*. For the latter book, the first review we received scolded us for not offering a chapter on the Kahiki. We didn't want to disappoint again, so we offer this modified version of Doug's original piece from 2012.

The classic "lost" Columbus restaurant for so many of us will always be equated with the crazy billboard at Hamilton and Livingston Avenue that would mechanically "wink" at me every Sunday morning when my parents drove us from our home in the Huber subdivision of Reynoldsburg to Brookwood Presbyterian Church in Bexley. The Polynesian Princess on the billboard beckoning me to join her for exotic pleasures on East Broad Street scared the devil out of me, and I would duck down behind the seat of my parents' station wagon for fear she would see me. Little did I know how that blinking mystery girl would find her way into the hearts of hundreds, if not thousands, of Central Ohioans. Of course, I am writing about the late great Kahiki.

The mother ship of all South Seas–themed restaurants was located at East Broad Street and Napoleon across from the Desert Inn (and one-time Playboy Club). It was shaped like a Polynesian fighting boat forty feet tall with giant flaming Moai heads outside the main doors that opened up into a tropical rainforest and reproduction of a typical Pacific Islander tribal village.

The Kahiki, whose name literally translates as "Sail to Tahiti," according to an undated Kahiki pamphlet, has its roots in another of Columbus's most venerated restaurants: the Top Steakhouse. Lee Henry and Bill Sapp had been operating the Top for three years when, in 1957, they thought that Columbus could support another supper club and began traveling around the country in search of inspiration. In their travels, it struck them that all of the Polynesian restaurants they visited were doing very well and offered a more casual experience than many of the other clubs of the era. Thus, the idea of the Kahiki began to take shape. (In large part, the Mai-Kai of Fort Lauderdale served as the most direct inspiration. Still in operation as of this writing, the entrance and locale can readily be seen as a blueprint for the construction and operation of the Kahiki.)

The pair hired Coburn Morgan to oversee the design and decorations of the Kahiki and architects Ned Eller and Ralph Sounik of Design Associates. The real estate housed a previous tiki bar they owned called the Grass Shack that had burned down. Construction began in June 1960 at a cost of over $1 million, and the Kahiki opened its legendary doors in February 1961.

The design of the building was based on men's meeting houses of New Guinea, and the details featured along the curved roof were found on many of the war canoes of the region. Pelicans and fish, thought to be symbols of plentiful good food, lined the apex of the roof. Two replicas of the Easter Island heads—Moai—stood guard at the doorway that was lined with murals to ward away evil spirits. Shell washbasins were found in the bathrooms, and "Thunder and Lightning" occurred in the tropical rainforests that lined the sides of the village interior. Also featured were giant wall-sized aquariums filled with tropical fish of the South Pacific.

The Outrigger and Maui bars were on either side of the foyer, and often the Beachcomber Trio could be found playing a fusion of Latin jazz and Polynesian melodies. The trio players were Bob Chalfant on piano; Henry Burch on vibraphone, conga, bells and trumpet; and Marsh Padillo on guitar, flute and percussion. In 1965, they cut a record; it was recently released in vinyl by Dionysous Records.

According to a pre-opening Kahiki pamphlet: "Most of the cocktail waitresses are the wives of servicemen or ex-servicemen and all are from

Japan or Korea. Although none of them had experience in this type of work, they were all trained rigidly for a two-month period prior to the Kahiki opening in February."

Patrons were immersed in a total world of the South Seas and, while there, could order their choice of exotic fare and island drinks. The Kahiki offered up such drinks as Malayan Mist, Blue Hurricane, Instant Urge, Maiden's Prayer, Misty Isle, Jungle Fever, Head Hunter, Zombie and the Smoking Eruption. Each one of these cocktails had its own sculpted mug designed just for the drinker, who could then purchase it from the gift shop and take it home as a souvenir. (Mrs. Sapp herself made the original ashtrays and mugs for the Zombie!) The various bars of the Kahiki used up to one thousand pineapples and two thousand bottles of rum monthly to keep up with demand.

As amazing as all these drinks sound, the most recollected Kahiki drink had to have been the Mystery Drink, which was made to serve four people and contained eight ounces of rum and brandy. Served in a bowl with a smoking volcano in the middle, it was served by the "mystery girl," who ceremoniously danced it to your table after being summoned by a giant gong. The service of this drink was meant to symbolize an ancient sacrificial ritual that supposedly stopped volcanoes from erupting. According to legend, the maiden chosen for the sacrifice was usually the chieftain's daughter. After several days of ceremony, feasting and luaus, the young lady would climb the volcano and fling herself into its crater—yikes! At the Kahiki, this was altered to have the mystery girl present the drink to the main tiki in the restaurant, and then, after bowing to the idol, she would bring the smoking bowl to the diners and present it to them, along with a lei of orchids, which were flown in two to three times a week from Hilo, Hawaii.

The Kahiki was also a draw for visiting celebrities, including Milton Berle, Andy Williams, Robert Goulet and, famously, Zsa Zsa Gabor, who allegedly ordered milk, of all things!

But all the mystery girls, leis, pineapples and celebrities couldn't keep pace with the march of time, and the Kahiki went through a slew of owners. In 1988, Michael Tsao took over complete ownership. In 1995, he began a frozen food company to market Kahiki in grocery stores.

In 1997, the building was put in the National Register of Historic Places, but on June 30, 2000, it was sold to Walgreen's corporation. The doors were shut forever on August 25, 2000. The demolition crew literally had to open up the roof to get the large tiki fireplace out.

Stacia Martin with Kahiki Moai fireplace. *Courtesy Todd Popp.*

As of this writing, a dozen-plus years have passed, and still the spell cast by the Kahiki remains powerful—so much so that the fine folks of the Columbus Food League have opened their own Polynesian-themed supper club, Grass Skirt. Fittingly, the Fraternal Order of the Moai, Kahiki Chapter, recently won the interior fountain of the Landmark restaurant. Fondly dubbed "Pete the Pig," as the fountain resembles a large boar, it now stands guard in front of the Grass Skirt and allows all who venture there to partake in some of the magic that was the Kahiki!

RECIPES

Ziggy's Brioche Dough

This recipe was used at Ziggy's for all its en croute recipes, like coulibiac.
Best Recipes of Ohio Inns and Restaurants, compiled by Margaret Guthrie (Amherst Press, 1988)

2 cups milk
¾ pound butter
¼ cup sugar
2 tablespoons dry yeast
3 eggs, room temperature
4 teaspoons salt
8 cups flour
3 tablespoons vegetable oil

In a heavy saucepan, bring milk, butter and sugar to a boil.

Remove from heat and cool to lukewarm. Put mixture in a large mixing bowl and mix in the yeast completely. Let stand for 10 minutes. Yeast will "proof"—that is, bubble up—indicating that it's active. Beat the eggs, which are at room temperature, and add to the mixture in the bowl along with the salt. Blend well. Add the flour, one cup at a time, until you have added seven cups. Mix until the dough pulls away from the side of the bowl.

Sprinkle the last cup of flour on a table or pastry board. Put the dough on the flour and knead in the last cup of flour until the dough is thoroughly mixed. The dough should be elastic and smooth.

Place the dough in a bowl oiled with the vegetable oil; turn to coat completely. Place the bowl in the warmest area of the kitchen. Cover with a clean cloth, as this prevents a skin from forming. Let rise until triple in size. Punch down and knead for 2 minutes; return to bowl and let rise again until double in size.

Punch down dough and prepare to roll out individual brioche or one large one. To roll one large brioche, take ¾ of the dough and roll with floured hands to form one large roll. Take the remaining ¼ of the dough, shape into a roll also, then make it pear-shaped. With your finger or a chopstick, poke a hole down in the center of the larger roll and insert the slender end of the pear-shaped piece of dough until it is joined.

To make smaller brioche, simply do the same thing, rolling each one with the palm of one hand and placing in small fluted brioche molds. Top the same way. Cover with a clean cloth and set in a warm place to rise.

Preheat oven to 425 degrees. When the dough has risen by one-third, brush the tops with beaten egg, being careful not to flatten the little tops. Place in the oven and bake for 20 to 25 minutes, watching to see that the bread doesn't brown too quickly. To test for doneness, insert the thin blade of a knife under the top. If it comes out clean, the bread is done. Do not unmold until cool.

Rigsby's Sourdough Bread

Starter:

¾ pound flour
1 ½ tablespoons sugar
½ ounce dry yeast
2¾ cups water

Bread:

2¾ cups water at 40 degrees
1 ½ cups starter
½ ounce salt
2¾ pounds flour

For the starter, mix all the ingredients together and let stand at room temperature for 7 to 8 days. Leave uncovered the first 3 days, then cover for the last 4 to 5. Temperature should be 72 to 80 degrees.

For the bread, mix the water and starter by hand in a large mixing bowl. Add the salt, then the flour, mixing at medium speed. Let the dough reach room temperature and double in size.

Refrigerate overnight. Let the dough reach room temperature, then shape into loaves. Cover and let rise in a warm place. Preheat oven to 400 degrees. Bake 35 to 45 minutes. Yield: 2 two-pound loaves.

Venison Paté with Cumberland Sauce from Ziggy's Continental

Best Recipes of Ohio Inns and Restaurants, compiled by Margaret Guthrie (Amherst Press, 1988)

Venison Paté

4 ounces veal
5 ounces pork
6 ounces venison
5 ounces button mushrooms
3½ ounces apples
2 ounces onions
6 ounces chicken livers
8 ounces bacon
5½ ounces fatback
1 teaspoon minced garlic
5 juniper berries
pinch fresh black pepper
1 teaspoon salt
1 tablespoon Madeira
1 tablespoon brandy
¼ cup egg whites
12 slices good bacon
baker's twine

Cumberland Sauce

½ cup fresh lemon juice
½ cup fresh orange juice
julienne peels of 2 oranges and 2 lemons

1 pound red currant jelly
1 ¼ cups port wine
1 tablespoon English mustard
pinch cayenne pepper
pinch ginger

To make the Venison Paté

Grind the veal, pork and venison. Wash the fresh mushrooms and let drain. Peel and rough chop the apples and onions. On a grill or in a large skillet, sauté the chicken livers, bacon, fatback, mushrooms, apples and onions lightly—about 5 minutes over medium heat.

Grind the sautéed ingredients. Mince the garlic and crush the juniper berries and add to the mixture. Add the other seasonings, mix in the ground meats, then add the Madeira, brandy and egg whites and blend well.

Preheat oven to 300 degrees. Lightly pound the 12 slices of bacon and line the inside of a terrine, reserving two slices. Add enough forcemeat (the mixture you've just made) to fill half the mold. On a hard level surface, raise the mold about 6 inches and let it fall flat. This settles the mixture. Fill the rest of the mold, raise and let fall three more times to settle the top half. Fold over any excess bacon hanging out the edges of the top of the forcemeat. Cover the bacon with plastic wrap, put the lid on the terrine and tie down with baker's twine. Place the terrine in a water bath (bain marie) and bake in the oven until the internal temperature reaches 130 degrees. Yield 1 terrine.

To make the Cumberland Sauce

Mix the two juices and the julienne peels together in a nonreactive saucepan and cook together over low heat, reducing by half. Once reduced, remove from heat and let stand for 2 minutes. With a whip, blend the rest of the ingredients into the juice peel mixture. Yield enough for 1 terrine.

To serve paté with the sauce, pour a little sauce on each service plate and place a slice of venison paté on the sauce. Garnish with watercress or any fresh crisp green.

Ziggy's Continental Light Cream of Green Lentil Soup with Celery

Best Recipes of Ohio Inns and Restaurants, compiled by Margaret Guthrie (Amherst Press, 1988)

1 ½ cups green lentils
3 tablespoons unsalted butter
1 medium celery root, peeled and cut into 1-inch julienne
1 medium leek, white part only, cleaned and cut into ⅛-inch slices
2 shallots, coarsely chopped
1 clove garlic, mashed
salt and pepper, to taste
½ small bunch watercress, stems removed
juice of 1 lemon
3 tablespoons olive oil
2 slices white bread cut into ½-inch cubes
2 teaspoons Dijon-style mustard
1 tablespoon red wine vinegar
½ cup heavy cream

Wash and soak lentils overnight. Drain, set aside. Melt the butter in a large stockpot and add the celery root peelings, leeks, shallots and garlic. Cook over medium heat until just wilted, about 5 minutes.

Add lentils to the cooked vegetables and mix well. Pour in 1 ½ quarts water; season with salt and pepper. Bring to a boil. Reduce the heat to low and simmer for 1 hour. Add watercress leaves to soup during the last 5 minutes of cooking.

In the meantime, place the celery root julienne in a nonreactive saucepan filled with cold water. Add the lemon juice and bring to a boil. Cook until tender, about 10 minutes. Drain in a nonreactive sieve or colander and set aside.

In a medium skillet, heat olive oil until hot. Add the bread cubes and fry over high heat until uniformly brown, about 2 minutes. Drain on paper towels.

Working in batches, if necessary, pour soup into a food processor or blender and pour until creamy. Pass through a fine mesh sieve into a medium saucepan and bring to a simmer over low heat. Add the mustard and vinegar. Pour in the cream and season with salt and pepper. Add julienne of celery root. Serve with croutons and add additional cream, if desired. Yields 8 servings.

Rigsby's Onion and Garlic Soup with Toasted Brie Crouton

Note: veal bones may be difficult to locate but should be available at butcher shops upon request.

Best Recipes of Ohio Inns and Restaurants, compiled by Margaret Guthrie (Amherst Press, 1988)

Yield 4–6 servings.

4½ pounds veal leg bones cut into 2-inch pieces
2 large white onions, diced but not peeled
2 large carrots, diced but not peeled
2 ribs of celery, diced
¼ cup tomato paste
4 medium white onions, peeled and diced
1 ounce clarified butter
1 teaspoon minced garlic
2 ounces sherry
salt and pepper to taste
3–4 ounces brie, cut into 4–6 slices
4–6 slices sourdough bread

To prepare the stock, roast the veal leg bones at 475 degrees for 2½ hours or until well browned. During the last hour, add the first amount of onions, the carrots and celery to the roasting pan with the bones.

Remove the roasted bones and vegetables from the pan and deglaze the pan with enough water to liquefy the drippings from the pan. Place roasted bones, vegetables and deglazing liquid into a pot that is large enough so that the bones and vegetables will be only halfway to the rim. Add tomato paste and 4½ quarts of water, or enough to cover the bones and vegetables by 4 to 5 inches.

Bring the stock to a boil, then reduce to a simmer. Continue to simmer 8 to 10 hours, skimming frequently. Replenish with water as needed.

Strain stock through a fine sieve into a clean pot. Simmer until stock is reduced by half or until it yields 1½ quarts. Continue to skim broth throughout the entire process. At this point, stock may be used to complete the soup. It may also be refrigerated for 4 to 5 days or frozen for 2 to 3 weeks

To complete the soup, in a large pot sauté the second amount of onions in butter until translucent; add the garlic and continue to cook for 2 minutes. Add the stock and bring to a boil. Reduce to a simmer and remove any sediment. Reduce soup until it is slightly thickened. Season with sherry, salt and pepper.

To prepare the sourdough croutons, divide the slices of brie over the bread slices and broil briefly until the cheese melts.

Ladle soup into individual bowls, placing one crouton on top of each bowl of soup.

Charbroiled Marinated Chicken Breasts

Bryn Mawr

3 whole breasts of chicken

Lime Basil Marinade

1 cup vegetable oil
⅓ cup fresh lime juice
1 teaspoon basil
1 teaspoon parsley
¾ teaspoon salt
⅛ teaspoon black pepper
3 cloves garlic, minced
3 drops Louisiana-style hot sauce
½ teaspoon sugar

Combine all ingredients for the marinade in a bowl and mix thoroughly. Allow marinade to stand at room temperature for 15 minutes.

Next, clean, rinse and split chicken breasts in half. Place the marinade in a large glass bowl, add the chicken and mix well so all of the marinade is evenly distributed over the chicken.

Cover well. Place in refrigerator for 24 to 48 hours before charbroiling.

If baked is desired, preheat oven to 350 degrees. On the top of stove, in an open pan, brown the chicken on the outside quickly and place in the oven for 45 minutes. Baste with butter for a rich flavor.

Roasted Pork Medallions with Watercress Sauce

Bryn Mawr

Best Recipes of Ohio Inns and Restaurants, compiled by Margaret Guthrie (Amherst Press, 1988)

12 pork tenderloin medallions
¼ cup dry white wine
¼ cup butter
¼ cup finely diced onion
¼ cup flour
1 cup heavy cream
1 cup half-and-half cream
¾ teaspoon salt
⅛ teaspoon pepper
½ cup chopped watercress leaves
peanut oil
salt
pepper
flour

Ask the butcher to cut the pork medallions so they are the same size.

Place wine and butter in a heavy-bottomed 1-quart saucepan. Heat until boiling. Add the onions and cook until the onions turn clear. Remove the pan from the heat, add the flour and whisk until all the butter is absorbed into the flour mixture. Add the creams, season with salt and pepper and whisk briskly until the mixture returns to a boil. Add the watercress and remove from heat. Keep warm.

In a large sauté or frying pan, place a little peanut oil and heat until very hot. Season the pork with salt and pepper and dredge in flour. Place the floured and seasoned medallions in the pan and brown quickly on both sides. Be sure the medallions are cooked through. Transfer to a warm serving platter, cover with the sauce, garnish with vegetables, potatoes or rice and top with fresh watercress.

To improve the sauce, after the meat has been removed, add ½ cup of white wine to the sauté and whisk, deglazing just until the wine boils. Strain the wine from the pan into the sauce, whisking to integrate the deglazing liquid into the sauce and pour over the meat.

Classic Genoise

Bryn Mawr

Best Recipes of Ohio Inns and Restaurants, compiled by Margaret Guthrie (Amherst Press, 1988)

6 eggs
1 cup flour, sifted
pinch of salt
½ cup butter, melted and cooled
½ teaspoon vanilla
1 cup sugar

Butter and flour two 8- or 9-inch cake pans. Preheat oven to 375 degrees.

Place the eggs, still in the shell, in a bowl of hot tap water while assembling the remaining ingredients. Warming the eggs in the bowl will make it easier to achieve maximum volume in the finished product.

Place the flour and salt in a small bowl. Similarly, combine the butter and vanilla in their own container.

Rinse a large mixing bowl with hot water to warm it. Dry the bowl. Crack the warmed eggs into the warmed bowl while eggs are still warm. Add the sugar and beat on high speed until the mixture is light, fluffy and very pale (about 5 to 8 minutes). Using a rubber spatula, carefully fold flour in, not just a few strokes, although the flour will not be fully incorporated at this time. Then take the butter and vanilla mixture and completely incorporate all ingredients. It is important to avoid overmixing, as this will result in a flat cake.

Pour batter into prepared pans. Bake in the oven until the top is browned and the cake begins to pull away from the sides of the pan, about 25 to 35 minutes. Cool completely before turning out of pans.

For a chocolate genoise, replace ½ cup of the flour with ½ cup of unsweetened, powdered cocoa.

Chocolate Terrine

Ziggy's Continental

Best Recipes of Ohio Inns and Restaurants, compiled by Margaret Guthrie

(Amherst Press, 1988)

4 ounces semisweet chocolate

11 ounces bittersweet chocolate

1 cup strong coffee

7 eggs separated

12 ounces softened butter

⅓ cup cognac

1 orange, zest only

In the top of a double boiler, melt the two chocolates with the coffee. Whisk together until completely melted and blended.

Add 3 of the egg yolks; blend well. Slowly incorporate the butter, blending well. Add the rest of the egg yolks along with the cognac and orange zest. Blend well; remove from heat and let stand 5 minutes, stirring occasionally.

Whip the egg whites to stiff peaks. Carefully fold the stiffened egg whites into the chocolate mixture, using a rubber spatula. Do not overmix. Once the two mixtures are incorporated, pour into a mold and let stand in the refrigerator for at least 24 hours.

To unmold the chocolate terrine, place the mold in a warm water bath for about 30 seconds. Remove the mold from the water and invert onto a sheet pan lined with parchment paper. Slice and serve, garnished with candied orange peel or fresh raspberries.

Fennel, Red Onion, Jicama and Celery Compote

Rigsby's Cuisine Volatile

Best Recipes of Ohio Inns and Restaurants, compiled by Margaret Guthrie

(Amherst Press, 1988)

1 small–medium bulb fennel, diced

1 small red onion, diced

1 bulb jicama, peeled and diced

2 tablespoons olive oil

1 tablespoon garlic

¾ cup balsamic vinegar
salt and pepper to taste

Combine all ingredients except the balsamic vinegar and salt and pepper in a nonreactive saucepan. Cook over low heat for 45 to 60 minutes or until the vegetables are soft but not overcooked. Add the balsamic vinegar and seasoning; cook another 10 minutes.

Use this vegetable compote as a garnish by making a cordon around a piece of grilled fish, or use as a sauce or relish over fish.

Cuban French Toast

Explorer's Club
From Ricky Barnes

about ½ pound stale Italian loaf, not sliced
2 cups milk
⅓ cup sugar
pinch salt
Crusteez Pancake Mix
Crisco
powdered sugar
freshly sliced pineapple, blackberries, strawberries or any other in-season fruit

Cut stale bread into cubes. Mix milk, sugar and salt in good-sized mixing bowl. Add in cubed bread and allow the milk mixture to soak in completely.

Take Crusteez pancake mix and double the water to get it to the consistency of a crepe batter. Take cubes of bread, dip the bread in it and toss it around; some of the bread will come off, but that's fine.

Deep fry to a golden brown, or get a deep pan and get Crisco very hot to about ½ inch deep in the pan or more and fry cubes of bread until golden brown.

Remove from fryer. Serve in bowl or plate and sprinkle powdered sugar over it. Put freshly sliced fruit on top of Cuban French Toast. Serve with syrup if desired.

Fried Chicken

Clark's Dining Room
"Simply Clark's Dining Room"

12-inch iron skillet
cooking oil
gas oven (the recipe will not work with electric)
3-pound young fryer chicken (from White Feather Farm in Pataskala; buy splits and cut them up into pieces)
flour
salt
flour pan

Fill skillet halfway full with cooking oil and turn on the fire on the gas stove. Let oil heat until you hear a "pinging" sound.

Place all chicken on top of the flour in the flour pan with the skin side up and salt lightly. Dust chicken with flour on both sides and knock off excess flour by tapping on the side of the flour pan. Place chicken pieces in hot oil with skin side up (breasts and thighs). Chicken should start to fry immediately. (At Clark's, the chicken was arranged around the skillet with breasts and thighs around the edge and legs and wings in the middle.)

Check progress after about 5 minutes and then every few minutes until the edges of the chicken are brown.

Turn chicken when edges of breasts are golden brown. After a few minutes, check chicken again and continue to do so by lifting the breasts and thighs to see that they are getting golden brown but not burning or scorching. (Note: turn down the fire slightly at this point to control browning.)

After checking that breasts and thighs are golden brown, turn them over. (Note: to check that breasts and thighs are done, puncture with a fork. If white liquid comes out, they are "milking" and should be back over on the skin side for a few minutes to finish.)

Turn off fire when all chicken is cooked.

Remove pieces from skillet onto paper-lined drop pan. After chicken is removed, with two hands carefully and slowly tilt the skillet to the side to drain the hot oil into the drain pan.

Tom Callaghan's Grilled Sirloin Steak with Banana Pepper Chili Pepper Butter

Betty Rosbottom

½ cup (1 stick) unsalted butter, cut into small pieces
scant ½ teaspoon salt
2 tablespoons finely chopped banana chili peppers (see note below)
2 teaspoons lemon juice
1 tablespoon chopped parsley

Place all ingredients in the bowl of a food processor fitted with a metal blade. Process several seconds until all ingredients are well blended. Mixture should be smooth and fluffy. Remove mixture to a small serving bowl and leave at room temperature if using within 3 to 4 hours. If you wish to make butter a day ahead, cover and refrigerate, but bring to room temperature before using.

Note: Banana chili peppers are pale yellow, slender and 4 to 5 inches long. They are available in many groceries today. To prepare for chopping, cut off the stem ends and slice the peppers lengthwise. Wearing rubber gloves, hold the halves under cold running water and scrape out the seeds. Dry the peppers and chop finely. You will need 2 to 3 peppers depending on size.

Steak and Garnish

1 prime-quality boneless sirloin steak, about 1½ inches thick (about 2 pounds)
3 medium sweet purple onions, peeled and cut lengthwise into quarters and placed on metal skewers
vegetable oil
salt and freshly ground black pepper

Prepare an outdoor charcoal grill or an indoor grill. When grill is ready, brush the meat and the skewered onion quarters generously with vegetable oil and place on the grate. Cook the meat, turning several times, until desired doneness. (Medium rare works well for this dish.) Cooking time will depend on the type of grill used and the intensity of the heat. The onions should cook in approximately the same time as the meat. They should be softened but still crisp. Remove if they finish cooking before the steak. When meat is done, remove from grill and place on a warm serving platter. Remove the onions from the skewers and arrange around the meat.

Salt and pepper the steak. Cut the meat into serving portions. (If you prefer, cut the steak into 4 serving portions before grilling.) Garnish each steak with a generous dollop of the seasoned butter. Makes 4 servings.

Poached Eggs on Black Bean Cakes

Owner/Chef Kent Rigsby, Rigsby's Cuisine Volatile

This unusual dish is full of flavor and intrigue. The beurre blanc sauce adds a rich, buttery taste to the well-seasoned cakes. The puréed beans, which can be prepared well in advance, also can be used in the appetizer recipe that follows.

2 cups black turtle beans
vegetable oil
½ cup yellow onion, diced
1 jalapeño pepper, diced (seeds included)
⅛ teaspoon garlic, minced
chicken stock (optional)
1 ½ teaspoons ground cumin
½ teaspoon ground coriander
salt and pepper to taste
flour
poached eggs
Banana Chili Beurre Blanc (recipe follows)

Soak black beans in cold water to cover overnight. (Or use quick-soak method: bring water and beans to a boil for 2 minutes, then cover and let stand 1 hour.) Drain and rinse beans.

In 1 tablespoon oil, sauté onion, jalapeño pepper and garlic until tender. Add to beans in a large saucepan. Cover with chicken stock or water. Bring to a boil, reduce heat, cover and simmer until beans are tender, 1 ½ to 2 hours. Drain, reserving broth.

Place drained beans in food processor or blender, in batches if necessary. Add cumin, coriander, salt and pepper and process until puréed, adding reserved liquid as needed if mixture appears too dry. (Mixture should be thick.) Transfer to shallow bowl, cover and refrigerate until cold.

Using ¼ cup of mixture, shape into patties. Dust both sides of patties lightly with flour. Sauté in hot oil in a frying pan, gently turning once, until cakes are slightly browned and heated through.

Place a poached egg on each bean cake. Top with Banana Chili Beurre Blanc. Makes 14 cakes. (If desired, leftover puréed beans can be used in Mexican Sushi recipe that follows.)

Per serving with Beurre Blanc: 355 calories, 26 gm. fat, 249 mg. cholesterol, 204 mg. sodium without added salt.

Banana Chili Beurre Blanc

½ cup dry white wine
1 ½ teaspoons shallot, minced
1 ½ ounces banana chili peppers, finely julienned and seeded (scant ¼ cup)
1 ½ teaspoons whipping cream
½ pound (2 sticks) butter, chilled, cut into 16 pieces
dash fresh lemon juice
salt and pepper to taste

Place wine in a saucepan with shallot and ¼ of the chili pepper strips. Bring to a boil and boil until wine has almost totally evaporated. Add cream and reduce heat to very low.

Add butter, 1 piece at a time, whisking constantly, adding more butter only after previous piece has been completely incorporated. Do not let mixture get too hot or sauce will separate.

When all the butter is incorporated, strain sauce through a fine sieve. Season with lemon juice and salt and pepper to taste. Add remaining chili pepper strips. Hold sauce at a very low temperature. (Do not make ahead and reheat.) Makes about 1 cup.

Mexican Sushi

Rigsby's Cuisine Volatile

about 1 cup leftover black bean purée from Black Bean Cake recipe
4 8-inch flour tortillas
salsa (recipe follows)

Spread a thin layer of bean purée (about ¼ cup) over each flour tortilla. Spread a thin layer of salsa (about 2 tablespoons) over the beans. Gently roll the tortillas as tightly as possible. Trim off both ends, then slice each roll into 6 portions. Makes 24 appetizers.

Salsa

1 cucumber, peeled, seeded and finely diced
½ sweet red pepper, finely diced
½ green pepper, finely diced
½ small red onion, finely diced
¼ teaspoon garlic, minced
1 tablespoon cilantro, chopped
1 ½ teaspoons red wine vinegar
juice of 1 lime
salt and pepper to taste
hot pepper sauce to taste (optional)

Combine all ingredients, mixing well. Cover and refrigerate until needed. Makes about 2 cups.

Dan Otanicar's Stuffed Pork Shoulder Roast

Whole World Bakery

1 3½- to 4½-pound boned pork shoulder roast
salt and pepper
1 pound fresh spinach
1 ½ pounds ricotta cheese
2 hard-cooked eggs, chopped
½ pound fresh mushrooms, sliced
2 cloves garlic, minced

If roast has not been cut all the way across to remove the bone, slice through the meat horizontally so that it can be laid open and flat. Pound meat to flatten it more. Sprinkle with salt and pepper.

Wash spinach and remove large stems. Place in a large pan with only the water that clings to the leaves. Cover and cook, stirring once or twice, just until spinach is wilted. Drain, squeeze dry and chop. In medium bowl, combine spinach, cheese, eggs, mushrooms and garlic.

Pat mixture over meat. Bring ends of meat together, enclose filling and tie in several places with string. (You may have to remove some of the filling to get the meat closed around it.)

Place roast in shallow roasting pan and roast at 350 about 25 to 30 minutes per pound or until internal meat thermometer registers 160. Let roast stand a few minutes before slicing. Makes 8 to 10 servings.

Whole World Bakery Brown Bread

1 pint milk
½ cup dark brown sugar, firmly packed
½ cup molasses
3 tablespoons vegetable shortening, such as Crisco, melted
3 cups whole-wheat flour
½ cup unbleached flour
1 teaspoon baking powder
1 teaspoon baking soda
1 teaspoon salt

Stir all ingredients together and bake in a greased loaf pan for 1 hour at 350 degrees.

Linguine Diablo

Bexley's Monk, courtesy Diane McCloy

3 tablespoons olive oil
2 boneless chicken breasts cut into strips
1 shallot, finely diced
2 cloves garlic, minced
½ cup white wine
½ cup chicken stock (homemade is preferred)
2 tablespoons Dijon mustard
1 cup heavy cream
fresh basil, crushed red pepper flakes, chopped parsley, freshly grated parmesan reggiano and salt and pepper to taste
1 pound linguine pasta

In a medium skillet over medium-high heat, add olive oil until hot. Add the chicken strips and saute until golden brown.

Add shallots and garlic to chicken and stir. Deglaze with the white wine, and then add the chicken stock and reduce by two-thirds. Add the Dijon mustard and heavy cream. Season to taste with crushed pepper and salt and pepper. At the last moment, add fresh basil.

Prepare the pasta according to directions on the package and toss with the sauce.

Plate the linguine and top with parmesan and parsley. Serve immediately.

BIBLIOGRAPHY

Alexander, Maria. Phone interview, June 2, 2017.

Bacha, Sarah Mills. *Columbus Dispatch*, January 9, 1994.

Barnes, Ricky. Multiple phone interviews, April 2017.

Bexley News. "Touchstone Café Opens." July 11, 1990.

Blake, Tom. *Prime Rib & Box Cars: Whatever Happened to Victoria Station?* Dana Point, CA: Tooter's Publishing, 2006.

Brockway, Chance. *Buckeye Lake*. Charleston, SC: Arcadia Publishing, 2005.

Brockway, Sonny. Phone interviews, May 27 and 28, 2017.

Capuano, Chuck. Phone interview, June 7, 2017.

Chenoweth, Doral. "Anatomy of a Restaurant." *Columbus Dispatch*, September 21, 1986.

———. "Café Rigsby Closing Doors Tonight." *Columbus Dispatch*, January 11, 2003.

———. "Captain Niki Planning New Wharf in Bexley." *Columbus Dispatch*, December 29, 1997.

———. "Captain's Back, Casting a Wide Net." *Columbus Dispatch*, May 7, 1998.

———. "Chalkias Family's Tale Is a Fish Story with Happy Ending." *Columbus Dispatch*, June 7, 1999.

———. "Changing Menus Add Flavor to Columbus," *Columbus Dispatch*, January 8, 1987.

———. *Columbus Dispatch*, November 10, 1988.

———. *Columbus Dispatch*, July 25, 1991.

———. *Columbus Dispatch*, August 1, 1994.

———. *Columbus Dispatch*, January 8, 1996.
———. *Columbus Dispatch*, July 22, 1996.
———. *Columbus Dispatch*, February 8, 2005.
———. "Dagwood May Enjoy Dagwoodz, a Short North Pub with Grub." *Columbus Dispatch*, March 4, 1999.
———. "Del Matto's Ownership Passes to Third Generation." *Columbus Dispatch*, November 19, 2002.
———. "First Anniversary Finds Rigsby's a Winner." *Columbus Dispatch*, February 26, 1987.
———. "Frezno to Close First Location, Open New One Downtown." *Columbus Dispatch*, June 17, 2003.
———. "The Grumpy Gourmet—Eclectic Menu Helps 'Frezno' Make a Name for Itself." *Columbus Dispatch*, July 6, 1995.
———. "High-Priced Liberty's Going on the Block." *Columbus Dispatch*, November 7, 2000.
———. "K2U to Close—New Ownership, Name Planned." *Columbus Dispatch*, December 17, 2002.
———. "Last Course Should Be First at Niki's Deli." *Columbus Dispatch*, September 26, 1985.
———. "Lost Planet's Thin-Crust Pizza Simply Out of This World." *Columbus Dispatch*, August 22, 1996.
———. "A Matter of Taste." *Columbus Dispatch*, September 18, 1992.
———. "New Short North Restaurant to Get Couple off the Streets." *Columbus Dispatch*, August 1, 1994.
———. "Out but Not Down." *Columbus Dispatch*, March 5, 2005.
———. "Peasant Rich in Imaginative, Tasty Cooking." *Columbus Dispatch*, August 29, 1985.
———. "Rigsby's Extends Short North Lease until 2010." *Columbus Dispatch*, September 4, 2004.
———. "Rigsby's Gaining Talent of Owner's Former Mentor." *Columbus Dispatch*, July 27, 1998.
———. "Set Sights on Blind Monk." *Columbus Dispatch*, February 13, 1986.
———. "Whole World Has a Lot of Talent." *Columbus Dispatch*, January 15, 1987.
———. "Wine Featured on Eight-Dinner Culinaire Program." *Columbus Dispatch*, September 22, 1988.
Christensen, Jon. "Captain Hauls in Tempting Specials." *Columbus Dispatch*, August 29, 2002.
———. "Rebirth of Seafood Favorite Does Reputation Proud." *Columbus Dispatch*, January 27, 2011.

Chronister, Bill. "Chef's Focus Is on Details, New Ventures." *Columbus Dispatch*, August 19, 2008.

Columbus Business First. "Developer Says Florentine in Franklinton Could Become New Restaurant." January 3, 2017. www.bizjournals.com/columbus.

Columbus Dispatch. "At Galaxy Café, a Little Light Sometimes Goes a Long Way." February 2, 1995.

———. Flippo ad, August 3, 1977.

———. "Guests Give Thanks for Country Cooking" (The Inn of Mount Gilead). November 18, 1981.

———. Midweek food section, Flippo ad, August 3, 1977.

———. "Program Legacy Dinner: Ziggy Honored at Refectory." March 21, 2015.

———. September 23, 1987; January 3, 1991; February 20, 1992; April 7, 1994; July 24, 1995; March 20, 1996; June 23, 1997; January 24, 2001; September 28, 2001; January 25, 2005; June 29, 2006; December 26, 2006; July 27, 2010; February 28, 2012; May 24, 2012; October 14, 2014.

Cosentino, Augustine M. Phone interview, March 17, 2017.

Darbee, Jeff. "City Quotient." *Columbus Monthly*, March 24, 2015, and February 2017.

Dawson, Sue. "Chefs Spill the Beans." *Columbus Dispatch*, March 6, 1991.

———. "Specialties of the House." *Columbus Dispatch*, May 10, 1987.

Delaware Gazette. "Brown Jug Marks 60 Years." April 22, 2006.

———. "Cookbook to Revive Brown Jug's Dishes." January 2, 2013.

———. "Landmark Closes Doors Abruptly after 62 Years." July 8, 2008.

———. "Restaurant to Open at Former Brown Jug Site." October 30, 2012.

Delaware News. "Brown Jug to Serve 5 Millionth Meal." April 27, 2005.

———. "Proud to Serve." February 7, 2000.

Dilley, Melissa. "Holding Court at the Florentine." *200 Columbus*. City of Columbus, 2012, 60.

Dominianni, Andy, and Erin Dominianni. *Columbus Italians.* Charleston, SC: Arcadia Publishing, 2011.

Douglass, Gale. Multiple interviews, 2017.

Eastside Messenger. "Restaurant Marks 25 Years with Closing." February 25, 1985.

Eichenberger, Bill. "Trio Trying for Hit at Short North Club." *Columbus Dispatch*, March 29, 1991.

Food for Thought (newsletter of the Brown Jug Restaurant). "The 'Jug' Celebrates 60 Years!" 1, no. 4 (April 2006).

Gabrenya, Frank. *Columbus Dispatch*, June 21, 1987.

Gandee, Bret. Phone interview, April 25, 2017.

George, Becky. Phone interview, April 17, 2017.

Godbey, Marty. *Dining in Historic Ohio.* Kuttawa, KY: McClanahan Publishing, 1987.

Gordon, Mark. Phone interview, May 2, 2017.

Grossberg, Michael. "The Changing Short North." *Columbus Dispatch*, March 1, 1998.

Gusset, Dale. Interview, March 17, 2017.

Guthrie, Margaret E. *Best Recipes of Ohio Inns & Restaurants.* Amherst, MA: Amherst Press, 1988.

Hayes, Ben. "Boy-Girl." *Columbus Citizen-Journal*, February 11, 1971.

———. "Expansion." *Columbus Citizen-Journal*, March 11, 1971.

Hays, Jim. "At Jim's You Get the Best." *Springfield News-Sun*, April 29, 1979.

Hedges, Charles. Phone interview, April 26, 2017.

Herb, Donna. Multiple phone interviews, April 2017.

Italian Heritage. Columbus, OH: Grandview Heights/Marble Cliff Historical Society, 1985.

Jeffries, Anna. "After Three Years Sparta Seeking Community Support." *Newark Advocate*, February 5, 2016.

———. "Sparta Serves Up Breakfast and Lunch with a Purpose." *Newark Advocate*, March 15, 2016.

Kanatas, Mary Beth. Personal interviews, March 22 and 29, 2017.

Kanatas, Ted. Phone interview, March 30, 2017.

Kasotis, George. Phone interviews, May 14 and 28, 2017.

Langstaff, Charles, and Grace Langstaff. Multiple interviews, 2016–17.

Lawlis, Barrett. "Sparta Looks for Aid One More Time." *Newark Advocate*, September 26, 2016.

Lindeboom, Walt. Phone interview, February 17, 2017.

Loeffler, Jim. Personal interview, March 2, 2017.

Lynch, Sandy Bean. Phone interview, March 14, 2017.

Malone, JD. "Restaurateur Rigsby Files for Bankruptcy." *Columbus Dispatch*, December 17, 2016.

Mardas, Suzanne Kanatas. Phone interview, April 7, 2017.

Marshall, John. "Critic John John Marshall Recalls the Glory Days of Rigsby's Kitchen, and How This Short North Pioneer Changed the Way Our City Eats." *Columbus Monthly*, January 19, 2016.

McCloy, George, and Diane McCloy. Interview, March 1, 2017.

Melvin, Sue Snouffer Kuhn. Multiple interviews, 2016–17.

Miller, Martha Johnson. Multiple personal interviews, 2017.

Miller, Phylis. Personal interview, March 18, 2017.

Miller, Tim. Phone interview, April 26, 2017.

Moras, Elizabeth. Personal interview, May 1, 2017.

Owens, Carmen. Multiple interviews, May 2017.

Park, Karen Kanatas. Phone interview, March 31, 2017.

Paul, Jim Girves. Phone interview, May 2, 2017.

Pedon, Felix. Phone interview, May 14, 2017.

Reynoldsburg Little Weekly. "Luncheon Visitors." March 28, 1962.

Richland Source. "Bellville Restaurant Gets New, Old Makeover." August 29, 2013.

Riepenhoff, Jill. "Geese Flock to Refuge." *Columbus Dispatch*, January 7, 1987.

———. "Neighbor News." *Columbus Dispatch*, October 11, 1989.

Rosbottom, Betty. "Local Restaurant Steak Tops on-the-Road Meals." *Columbus Dispatch*, April 23, 1986.

Rose, Marla Matzer. *Columbus Dispatch*, June 22, 2010.

Ruth, Robert. "Café Training Disabled Has Money Trouble." *Columbus Dispatch*, May 6, 1991.

Saha, Anand, and Doris Saha. Mozart's website. mozartscafe.wordpress.com.

Seman, Gary, Jr. "Flatiron Overhauls Menu after Testing." *Columbus Dispatch*, n.d.

———. *This Week Community Newspapers* (Columbus, OH), February 20, 2014.

———. *This Week Community Newspapers* (Columbus, OH), April, 2017.

Smola, Jennifer. "Sparta Closes." *Columbus Dispatch*, July 29, 2016.

Snyder-Lucas Family History. San-Dar Smorgasbord website. snyderfamilyhistory.wordpress.com.

Stallings, Beth. *Columbus Crave*, November 9, 2015.

———. "Whole Lotta Chutzpah." *Columbus Crave*, Fall 2015.

Stover, Steve, and Jon Christensen, eds. *Zagat Survey: Ohio Restaurants.* New York, 1994.

Stuckey, Sue. Personal interview, May 20, 2017.

Trowbridge, Denise. "Couple Sells Earlier Restaurants to Settle on Their Newest Venture—And to Work Together." *Columbus Dispatch*, May 14, 2013.

———. "Husband, Wife with Plenty of Local Restaurant Experience Open Zoe Café in Bexley." *Columbus Dispatch*, January 27, 2015.

———. "A New Chapter." *Columbus Dispatch*, October 29, 2013.

———. "A Post-Fire Comeback—Whole World Dishing Up Vegan, Vegetarian Fare." *Columbus Dispatch*, July 6, 2010.

Turner, Tracy. "Barrel 44 Expands into Bexley Monk's Space." *Columbus Dispatch*, January 5, 2012.
Webb, David. Phone interview, April 26, 2017.
Westerville in Focus. "Williams Grill: 80 Years of Fine Dining and Fun."
Westerville Public Opinion & News. "Matriarch of Old Williams Grill Dies." May 5, 1995.
———. October 28, 1994, and October 4, 1995.
———. "Restoration of Williams Nears Completion." May 4, 1972.
Wiley, Jack. "Club's Owner Really Cookin.'" *Columbus Dispatch*, February 19, 1990.
———. "Monk Revived Gets New Name." *Columbus Dispatch*, December 21, 1987.
———. "Saturday Is Swan Song for 'Captain Mike.'" *Columbus Dispatch*, May 27, 1993.
Wilson, Gary. "Local Restaurant Serves Up a Piece of 'Brubaker' History." *Perry County Tribune*, September 30, 2009.
Wolf, Barnett. "Union Promises Food, Décor That's Worthy of Predecessor Zola." *Columbus Dispatch*, December 26, 2006.
Wolf, Ed. Phone interview, May 30, 2017.
Worthington News. "Hearth & Eagle Opens with New England Atmosphere." December 5, 1974.
Yee, Helen. Personal interview, September 26, 2016.

INDEX

C

E

F

G

H

I

J

K

L

M

N

O

P

Q

R

Y

Z

ABOUT THE AUTHORS

Doug Motz is the past president of the Columbus Historical Society (CHS) and continues to give tours of the core city for CHS and Columbus City Adventures. He is the coauthor of *Lost Restaurants of Columbus, Ohio* and *Kahiki Supper Club: A Polynesian Paradise in Columbus*. He writes a "History Lesson" column for the website columbusunderground.com and gives frequent local history quizzes on the local ABC affiliate WSYX's morning television program, *Good Day Columbus*.

Christine Hayes spent her childhood in Columbus restaurants while her father gathered tidbits for his *Columbus Citizen-Journal* columns, which she published in *The Ben Hayes Scrapbook*. Coauthor of *Lost Restaurants of Columbus, Ohio*, Christine assists in the Acorn Bookshop in Grandview, writes a column for the *Short North Gazette* and makes art cars and collage/assemblage as Ramona Moon. She graduated from UC Irvine in theater, taught Montessori school and lived in San Francisco for twenty-seven years before returning to Columbus.